HOW TO WRITE ONE SONG

JEFF TWEEDY

DUTTON

DUTTON

An imprint of Penguin Random House LLC
penguinrandomhouse.com

DUTTON and the D colophon are registered trademarks
of Penguin Random House LLC.

Song lyrics © Words Ampersand Music, administered by
BMG Rights Management.

LIBRARY OF CONGRESS CATALOGING-IN-PUBLICATION DATA

Names: Tweedy, Jeff, 1967– author.
Title: How to write one song / Jeff Tweedy.
Description: New York : Dutton, Penguin Random House LLC, 2020. |
Identifiers: LCCN 2020030553 (print) | LCCN 2020030554 (ebook) |
ISBN 9780593183526 (hardcover) | ISBN 9780593183533 (ebook)
Subjects: LCSH: Popular music—Writing and publishing.
Classification: LCC MT67 .T94 2020 (print) | LCC MT67 (ebook) |
DDC 782.42/13—dc23
LC record available at https://lccn.loc.gov/2020030553
LC ebook record available at https://lccn.loc.gov/2020030554

Printed in the United States of America
1 3 5 7 9 10 8 6 4 2

BOOK DESIGN BY ASHLEY TUCKER

I'd like to dedicate this hopeful little book to all of the songs to come. Yours and mine. To all of those moments yet to unfold where we find ourselves awake to a possibility we hadn't anticipated. To all of the songs like windows, open just enough for us to make our escape, and to all of the songs like windows, closed and clear enough in a dim light to see our own reflection and be reminded of who we are. Not one of these songs to come will save any of us for very long. But keep writing and waiting and watching life as it reveals itself to us slowly over time. Each song and each act of creativity, indeed, is an act of defiance in a world that often feels determined to destroy itself. The songs we have yet to write will always be more important than the songs we've already sung, and certainly more important than the songs we never bring to life. I hope you, dear reader, will take this book in the spirit it was written—as a humble request to write your one song today and tomorrow and each day after that. We have a choice—to be on the side of creation, or surrender to the powers that destroy.

CONTENTS

PART III

PART IV

INTRODUCTION

Songs are mysterious. Any idea where they come from? I've written tons and tons of songs and STILL the best I can think to say after I finish one I'm happy with is "How'd I do that?" It's confusing when you can DO something and not know exactly HOW you did it (and then somehow expect to do it again).

I think that's why so much mysticism gets attached to songwriting when people try to talk about it. You hear things like "I'm just a conduit" and "The universe wanted me to have this song." Whatever you say, man. I'm pretty sure it's still ME doing the work. Some partnership between my conscious mind and my subconscious gets results, but when things are going right, the distinctions between the two become blurry, and I'm never really sure which is in charge.

So the idea of teaching songwriting feels more like teaching someone how to think. Or how to have ideas.

Because songs, to me, are much more like individual thoughts than other works of art are. They're hard to hold on to—airlike and ephemeral. They pass through time. They're here, then gone . . . Yet they're portable, they can linger as a memory, and, even crazier, they can just pop into our minds for no discernible reason. Other art forms like paintings and books have physical shapes and permanence, but how many of them can you hum a few bars of?

Understandably, I think we all sort of assume songs are more conjured than written. And it makes sense that people are skeptical about the idea that songwriting can be taught. I mean, it's easy to see how a step-by-step approach might be applied to the "craft" of songwriting— music theory, traditional song shapes, meter—but in my experience, that's just the architecture. How do you teach someone to write the kind of song that makes someone *else* want to write a song? A song that you can fall in love with, and a song that feels like it's capable of loving you back. Can you teach that? I'm not sure.

But I have a feeling that part of the problem is the enormity of teaching someone how to write song*s*— plural. Instead, I believe that the only way to teach someone to write song*s* would be through teaching them how to give themselves permission to write ONE song. To teach them how to teach themselves—starting with one song.

To me, the difference between one song and song*s* is

not some cute semantic trick; it's an important distinc-
tion, and it's more precise about what you're actually doing. No one writes song*s*—plural. They write one song,
and then another. And it's also a reminder of what you
really want. Or what *I* think you should REALLY want,
which is to disappear—to watch your concept of time
evaporate, to live at least once inside a moment when
you aren't "trying" to do anything or be anything anymore. To spend time in a place where you just are.

OK? OK. That's all . . . That's something that doesn't
happen through song*s*—plural. It happens only when
you've lost yourself in the process of making one song.

PART I

1

Why?

Or Do You Need a Reason to Write a Song?

—— **Why I Write Songs** ——

Long before I wrote my first song, I thought of myself as a "songwriter." I would say to people, "Guess what? I'm a songwriter," not "I might like to try my hand at songwriting someday." Just "Yep, I'm a songwriter." It was bonkers! I think I was around seven years old. I was delusional. I was a delusional seven-year-old, and I had stumbled onto some internal TED Talk–level trick of self-actualization. It worked! It turns out that the reason I started writing songs is because I happened to be a songwriter. That, plus the looming sense as I got older that it would only be a matter of time before someone would say, "Boy, I'd love to hear one of your songs!" So I guess I found the desire to NOT be revealed as a complete fraud quite motivating as well.

Does that sound like you? Do you like the idea of

what it would feel like to be someone who writes songs? Is that your answer to the question "What do you want to be when you grow up?" Maybe minus the awkward transition from "I'm thinking firefighter . . . maybe cowboy . . . You know, I'd like to be something in the firefighting realm, but I'd also like to be on horseback if possible" to the crazy conviction of "Songwriter! Next question, Grampa!" Maybe your internal dialogue sounds something more like this: "I'd really like to be able to maybe write songs someday?" OK. Let me just settle this right off the bat: You are a songwriter! No doubt about it—and definitely as much as I was before I wrote any songs. Phew. I'm glad we got that out of the way. All right then, thanks for buying the book.

Just kidding. Ha! That was hilarious!

Sorry. I'm going to come at this from another angle, because I think it's as close to the core philosophy of this book as I can get, and I believe it's worth repeating in a way that might be understood from a broader perspective than just songwriting. The truth is that as I got older, the answer to "What do you want to be?" became much more difficult to say out loud. Even though I always had a pretty good idea that I wanted to write poems and songs and play music, I always had a hard time telling people that I wanted to be a poet or a songwriter or an artist. It still feels wrong sometimes to label myself as something so grand in my estimation. Why? Is it false modesty? I doubt it. My ego seems sturdy enough these days to tolerate some aggrandizement.

I think the disconnect is more related to the idea of "being" anything when it's the "doing" that's most rewarding. Being something isn't real in the same way that doing something can be real. Everyone has a different idea of a "songwriter." We all picture that differently. Your "songwriter" wears a beret, doesn't she? I knew it! If you can pull off a beret, you can definitely write songs. Anyway, my "songwriter" doesn't wear a beret or really think of himself as a songwriter at all unless he's writing a song. That's another main reason I wanted the focus on ONE song to be reflected in the title of this book. When you're in the act of creating, when you're actually focused on that one song, and that focus is allowing you to disappear (which we've already established is ideal and to be desired), there isn't anyone else's image of who you are to compete with. In fact, even the image you have of yourself can take a breather.

So You Want to Be a Star?

It's soul-crushing, at any job, to aspire to BE something versus being driven by what you want to DO. Do you want to be a "star"? Don't bother. You're going to lose. Even if you make it, you'll lose. Because you're never going to be exactly what you're picturing. But what do you want to do? You want to play music in front of people? You can do that. You want to see if you can get better at playing in front of a larger group of people? You might be able to do that. I can even see someone deciding that they're going to create an outrageous persona and experiment with new musical forms. And that might end up making them a rock star, but I doubt the title is anywhere near as satisfying as the creation part. Maybe it's a cliché, but you have to focus on verbs over nouns—what you want to do, not what you want to be.

Keep things simple. You want to be heard—listened to. We all do. So as stupid as it sounds, that only means you have to make a sound. Many songwriters have aspired to be Bob Dylan, including me. And is that an overambitious desire? Yes and no. Did I truly want to BE Bob Dylan? No. I wanted to do what Bob Dylan does, and on the most basic level there was nothing stopping me from doing what Bob Dylan does. That doesn't mean I can play the guitar or sing the same way or write songs the same way or as well. It just means that I make a sound. I write a song and I sing it. At the very least, I hear myself. If you're coming to me for inspiration because you want to sound like me or "be" me . . . well, I'm flattered. But you'll be surprised how good it feels to hear yourself sing your own song.

⸺ Will One Song Be Enough? ⸺

For some reason I feel the need to clearly explain how I distinguish between an "aspiration" and an "accomplishment." To me, "aspiration" is a word that is reserved for your loftiest goals, your dreams. I think "to aspire" is to aim for something just out of reach or something far away temporally—your end goal, maybe? It's more related to the idea of how you want your work to be acknowledged. An "achievement" can mean sort of the same thing, I suppose, but I would argue that an "achievement" is something clearly defined and attainable.

I think aspirations are great! And I think you should dream big. It's hard to do something you can't envision, so close your eyes and picture something wonderful every chance you get. But for now, let's just take a look at what you're trying to accomplish. Are you trying to create a body of work? Or could one song be enough? Just to see what it feels like to have your own song to sing?

Because one song is all it takes to make a connection. And in my opinion, connection is the loftiest of all aspirations. To my way of thinking, there isn't much else of any value going on in any song or work of art. At the core of any creative act is an impulse to make manifest our powerful desire to connect—with others, with ourselves, with the sacred, with God? We all want to feel less alone, and I believe that a song being sung is one of the clearest views we ever have to witness how humans reach out for warmth with our art.

I'm sure you've felt that as a listener, too. That warmth works both ways. We look for it in the art we choose—in the music we listen to. But how do you make a song do that? How can you be sure you're making that connection happen? I think that to get there we have to start with ourselves. And to connect with ourselves, I believe, requires an effort to tune in to our own thoughts and feelings through practice or habit.

Before my dad died, he asked me, "How old are you?" (Dad was never the most attentive father.) I told him I was fifty. He said, "That's great. The years between when I was forty-five and fifty-five were the most productive of my whole life." And I was thinking, "How was he productive?" My dad worked for the railroad his entire career. I guess he made improvements to the safety and productivity of the rail yard. Maybe he reconfigured the computers in the tower or something. He had a lot of expertise in electronics. And he looked at his career as having some productivity that he felt connected to.

But I've always wondered if he meant something else—it's really interesting how you recognize genetics and see yourself in your relatives and your family as you grow older. My father did have the impulse to sit down and write poetry. He would go to the basement from time to time when he was upset about something or when he was mad. He'd sit and write a poem, and then come upstairs, half drunk, and read a simplistic, heavily rhyming but not entirely artless poem about the Alton & Southern Railway, or our neighbor who'd died, or something else that he was stewing about.

We didn't have many books in our house; we hardly had any high-minded notions about who we were as a family, and for all I know, book reading might have been akin to putting on airs. Dad was a high school dropout. My mother was a high school dropout. But I think they were both brilliant—I mean, really fucking smart. At some point, my dad must have realized that there were things he needed to say that didn't mean as much or sound right without some rhyming. "Hmmm . . . a poem. I betcha I could write one of those." He probably wrote them at work, in his head. What's more curious is how he gave himself permission to do it. I think a lot of people write poems in their heads but don't give themselves permission to write them down or share them. I'm sure the beer provided some confidence—some internal urging and support that led to the late-evening recitals. But when he first sat down to write—it was always straight after work—he was sober as a judge and riding a wave of pure inspiration.

I want to be a person who encourages more humans to do that—to have some private moments of creativity, whether they share their creations or not. We should have an army of people advocating for that. I think it's the coolest thing in the world when someone steps outside their so-called station in life to indulge in a personal "art for the sake of art" moment. If we're being realistic about what an end goal should be, creating something with no ambition other than to get something off our chest might be the purest thing anyone could aim for.

2

The Hardest Part
Getting Started

— Put Yourself on the Path —

I happen to love deadlines. Not everyone does. I do, because they fit with my belief that art isn't ever really complete. As the saying goes, "No work of art is ever finished; it can only be abandoned in an interesting place." It's a little soon to delve into my particular routines, but at this point in my life, I write with such regularity that being given a deadline (for example, an exact date when an album needs to be delivered to the mastering lab) is basically a "pencils down" alarm bell that allows me to stop making up new songs and to spend some time whipping an LP's worth of tunes into shape. Maybe that's not the level of commitment we're shooting for here, at least not yet, since we are focused on just one song. At any rate, we're going to have to unlock what motivates you to get started. Knowing how to write a song isn't going to help you much if you never find the inspiration or discipline to get started.

I think I taught myself this lesson during the making of *Summerteeth*. We had finished the record and we were happy with it, but the execs at the label said to me literally the most clichéd thing anyone could ever picture a record exec saying: "We don't hear a single." So they wanted another song—"And this one better be good!" I'll spare you the deliberations that went on behind the scenes and my own annoyance about the whole thing. In my mind, every song I'd just delivered was a SOLID GOLD pop gem! But I lied and said, "Boy, I have just the song." That even though we'd just spent months making a record, I'd for some reason forgotten to mention the surefire hit I'd been keeping in my back pocket. In reality, I had no such song, of course, but I thought it'd be interesting, since they were paying for it, to fly to LA and pretend that I knew what a chart-scorching pop song sounds like. I wrote most of "Can't Stand It" on the plane.

It was the first time I confirmed for myself that inspiration wasn't always the first ingredient in a song. In this case it was demand. Eventually I found inspiration in the process and even felt good about taking their money to teach myself that lesson. The song didn't "chart," even though the label dudes claimed that they loved it and that they were going to give it the "Big Push." So it goes. The point is, when I say something like, "Inspiration is overrated," it's not because I think you don't ever need to be inspired. What I'm trying to tell you, and what I still tell myself frequently, is that inspiration is rarely the first step. When it does come out of the blue, it's glorious. But it's much more in your own hands than the divine-intervention-type beliefs we all tend to have about inspiration. Most of the time, inspiration has to be invited.

— Process —

To me, process is whatever act you can engage in, whatever steps you can take, and whatever device you have at your disposal that you can use, together, that reliably results in a work of art. "Process" is also the only name I know of for whatever series of contortions and mental tricks we have available to lose ourselves in when we create. It's the door to the disappearing that I've already described as my ultimate desired creative state—being able to get "gone" enough long enough for a song to appear. Beyond what it helps me create, disappearing is also the most sustaining part of what I do. And it's the part that's long over with way before a record comes out.

I've talked to other songwriters about this, and some have pointed out how it can also be a vital part of performing. How it's important to get to a place where you're confident enough to prevent your ego from overseeing every move and hiding your vulnerability. When I'm on stage, my experience often goes something like this: Blankness . . . bliss . . . blankness . . . twinkle of awareness that rocking has been achieved . . . bliss . . . Voice of Observing Ego yelling over amplifiers, WOW! YOU ARE FUCKING KILLING IT DUUUUDE! . . . Clang! Wrong chord.

My ego does that to me all the time. That's kind of having an ego in a nutshell. It's there to build you up. And protect you. To protect your idea of yourself as smart, and handsome, and someone who should be taken seriously and never be laughed at. Your ego wants to conceal your insecurity and your fear. And that's why it can be such an unwelcome intrusion when we're trying to create or perform. You need your human frailty to be at least somewhat visible if you want to connect on an emotional level—if you want things to feel real.

So that's why I surrender to process, why I so regularly employ the mental tricks that I'm going to talk about later in the book—the tricks that get me in the right frame of mind to create. It makes it easier to have moments of truth and recognition, and it gets my ego out of the way. And getting my ego out of the way makes it easier to listen to myself with some objectivity—to hear myself almost as a different person would. So if you can give yourself over to a process and get comfortable with disappearing, you're likely to harvest some hard-to-find truth along the way, both about yourself and about what you're trying to say.

Don't worry about your ego. It'll be fine taking the backseat for a while. Trust me, it's never gone for long. It'll be there to help figure out what to do with whatever you make, take credit for the parts people love, make excuses for any shortcomings, decide what font and point size to use on the poster, etc. In the end, learning how to disappear is the best way I've found to make my true self visible to myself and others.

Inspiration Versus Craft

Let's talk more about what we call "inspiration." It's overrated. Have we established that? As you know pretty well if you've read this far, I believe that you have to invite inspiration in. I've found that most people who have a fulfilling life in art are, like me, the people who work at it every day and put the tools of creation in their hands frequently, who not only invite inspiration in but also do it on a regular basis. Instead of waiting to be "struck" by inspiration, they put themselves directly in its path. Pick up a guitar, and you're much more likely to write a song. Pick up a pencil . . . etc.

There's little doubt in my mind that because I do so much of that planned, methodical thinking in which I put the tools of inspiration in my own hands—a guitar, a pencil, a computer—I've trained my subconscious to always be working a little bit. Because I've already cleared the pathway and tended that pathway, kept it open and remained receptive to it, by practice.

But beyond that, once you get started, how much is inspiration and how much is craft? The craftsman part of me understands that as a song crafter, I could probably be OK looking at it as if I were building tables. As if I were using a standardized process that will guarantee another song, and the pipeline of songs I'm committed, and driven, to provide. But I personally think that I am where I am because I aspire to make trees instead of tables. Because there's something higher in my mind about doing so. And that I've accepted the fact that it's also impossible to make the perfect tree—there's no perfecting it. There's no reaching some conclusion that you've made THE tree.

In some way it's very high-minded—putting you on the same plane as God. But on another level, it's letting you off the hook. A tree could be almost anything. A tree is basically just . . . me. I'm a tree. I didn't fit perfectly into any mold. I wasn't made by a specific set of plans. The things that have happened to me in my life have taken away some of those straight edges and shaped me into a tree, shaped me into something less predictable, less understandable.

— **What's Important When You're Getting Started** —

My sincere wish is for people to be able to foster a little more license to create in their own lives. I do sincerely want it for everyone. I understand that there are time considerations—people look at me and think that I work so hard, maybe because it's unusual in terms of people's conception of a rock musician, that I would work normal hours. But I think actually setting aside time to spend in the creative state—especially when I see how much time people spend on their phones—is something you can do every day. I think this suggestion is valuable even for people who juggle a mind-numbing load of obligations, to their kids, to work, to whatever else is important in their life. Even if you can only find five minutes—it doesn't take that long. It's just a matter of telling yourself that your creation is OK, no matter what it is.

3

Obstacles

What's Stopping You?

Now that you're a songwriter, we're going to have to answer some much more difficult questions and learn how to fend off some pretty nasty comments. No, I'm not talking about the internet (yet). The calls are coming from inside the house! Primarily, you're going to have to respond to the merciless interrogations that your doubts and insecurities are going to hit you with daily. Like "Who do you think you are?" and "Are you kidding me with this bullshit?" All the things you tell yourself to knock yourself down a peg.

Let's figure out how to deal with a few of the typical tropes of self-defeating inner dialogue. I'm convinced the dreams we have for ourselves go unattained from a lack of permission more than any deficit in talent or desire. And I'm going to stress again that when I say "permission," I mean the permission we withhold or give ourselves to pursue those dreams. Here are some examples of the big obstacles I think we often put in our own way.

— I Don't Have Time —

I know what you're thinking. How could I have time to write a song when I hardly have time to do the things that I'm REQUIRED to do? I'm almost positive this is a hurdle for anyone following a creative pursuit. It's real. There's only so much time in a day—I get it—but I think I should give it to you straight.

Nobody makes good choices when they aren't aware they're making a choice. First of all, let's look at how you're spending your time now. I believe most of us only spend time doing the things that we truly want to do. So if you're doing something with your free time other than writing a song, it's because you really don't want to write a song. I'm not going to give you some "Pull yourself up by the bootstraps" or "You could be the greatest songwriter in the world, you just have to work at it" type of bullshit. I don't believe that. I'm just saying that if you really wanted to write songs, you could find some time to get better at it. And getting better at it would most likely make you feel like spending your time making up songs.

It really is a choice that's being made. And if you recognize that you've made a choice to play Candy Crush for forty-five minutes or dive deep into a YouTube marble-racing rabbit hole, then maybe you could choose to spend that time strumming a guitar and finding a chord progression that inspires you instead. Or spend forty-five minutes freewriting. Frankly, even that much time isn't necessary. You don't have five minutes? You don't have three minutes? How long is a song? Three minutes? Obviously we're going to get into more nuanced instruction later, but for now, pick up a guitar and bang on it for three minutes. There, you've essentially written a song. That's honestly something that could make you feel better. Pick up a guitar and scream your fucking head off. That's going to make you feel better. And it's going to make you feel like you did the one step that you didn't think you'd be able to get yourself to do.

I want to give you tough love. If you think you want to write songs but you can't find time to do something as pleasurable and lovely as making up a song, then it's just an idea you want to have of yourself as a person who writes songs, but you've found other things that are more important to you. I suppose there are people who so adore the idea of themselves as something—songwriter, author, athlete, etc.—that they will actually torture themselves doing something displeasurable to maintain their self-perception. But I'm going to leave that aside for now, because I don't understand that mentality at all. I love writing songs, and I'm going to assume that when you picked up this book, you were at the very least curious to find out why.

— I Don't Know How or I Won't Make Anything Good —

Neither of those is true. You don't know how to write a song? If you've never tried, how do you know if you can write a song or not? OK, technically it may be true that you don't know how, but the point here is that not knowing how to do something is a poor excuse not to try. I can also say that, even after writing hundreds of songs, this feeling has never left me entirely. In fact, one of the reasons I advocate so strongly for maintaining some creative pursuits in life is my belief that not knowing exactly how something like a finished song comes together creates an incredible magical feeling that always leaves me satisfied and full of wonder. There's really no exact way to do it—it's not like putting together IKEA furniture. It's just about getting started on the right path. So let's not worry so much about *how* just yet. The rest of this book will provide you with some road maps to find your own particular *how*.

You don't think you can create anything that will sound like the traditional definition of a "good song"? OK. So technically this may be true as well. But what's "good"? Isn't it a little strange that we enjoy doing a lot of things in life without that type of good-versus-bad judgment? Do you ever toss a Frisbee? Does it ever enter your mind to stop when you realize you suck? I think it's natural that songs can come to feel sacred to us, and I suspect that the importance certain songs have to each of us is at the root of our hesitance to commit the unspeakable act of making a not-good song.

Trust me on this, though. A "bad" song isn't going to leave a permanent stain on your record. I know you're thinking of all the notable and specific cases (like, say, Rebecca Black's "Friday") where an artist is associated with one horrible atrocity of a song. But I would like to point out the "writing" of the song left no permanent mark—it was the sharing and promotion of said heinous work that did the damage. Anyway, I guarantee you that I have records made by people who are worse than you. Records that I enjoy. (Song-poem collections. Primitive early industrial noise cassettes!) Almost anything can be a song if it's a song to you. And almost anything can be a record, but that's a different topic.

Also, do you think everybody who writes songs started off great? That their songs were great? That is definitely not the case. You have to sound bad to sound good, even if you've written five hundred songs. Being willing to sound bad is one of the most important pieces of advice that I can give you. Writing a song will teach you that it's OK to fail. And more than that, that it's actually good to fail, and that you can come to appreciate the gifts of failure. Failure can be a kind of pain that you shouldn't let go to waste, at least as long as you're in the proper space mentally. It will help you deal with rejection in a lot of other areas of your life. The reaction I got from the Warner Bros. execs when we handed in Wilco's album *Yankee Hotel Foxtrot* has been well documented. We sent them mixes as they were completed, and they hated every one and claimed each was worse than the last, eventually dropping us before another label that was also part of Warner Bros. rebought the album. Right, you know that story. But the part that I don't think I've ever discussed is how liberating it was to realize I could survive the absolute worst-case scenario for an artist—being told directly, flat out "You suck!"

What an incredible gift that was. To my ears, our album had started off in a terrible place and only got better, until it ended up being something I was satisfied with. And once I listened to that version, the one I liked, it sounded like nothing I could have ever imagined without going through the process of it sounding wrong to me. Basically, the opposite experience the executives at Warner Bros. had described.

So who was right? It didn't really matter. We can all understand, intellectually, art is subjective, but that doesn't generally help much when our feelings get hurt. I remember the first time I listened to *Yankee* after they told me they hated it. I was kind of dreading it, because I thought that the toxicity, controversy, and hurt feelings about the album might have spoiled it somehow. But I listened, and nothing had happened to the record. Or me. In fact, what I kept thinking about was how glad I was we had changed it to what it had become. And as I listened, I was already starting to hear new songs and getting excited about different directions the band could go from where we had landed. When I woke up the next day and the day after that and kept finding myself in love with this thing we had made, I came to the conclusion that no one's judgment—theirs or mine—would ever hurt for very long, provided I could bring myself back to listening and loving. And looking out for the next song.

—— I Don't Know What to Write About ——

This one I get a lot, and so it's one that I've thought about a lot. I take it very seriously, because it reflects a deep concern people have: What do you care about? What do you talk to your friends about? Whatever is on your mind is a good-enough topic for a song, in my opinion. But let's go back to the central idea of this book. Creating something out of nothing is the important part. And maybe, like me, you'll discover that you're often better off learning how to write without much concern for what you're writing about. And through that process, you'll discover what is on your mind. "Jesus, Etc." was never about anything specific to me until I sang it live for the first time and learned how sincerely it conveyed my wish for a better sense of unity with my extremely devout Christian neighbors. So do some freewriting. Write without thinking. I'm sure there will be some things that will surprise you, along with some nonsense.

Maybe you'll write something that reminds you of a song you've heard before, but it'll feel like you discovered a new way to say it. Finding your voice is something we'll delve deeper into later, but for now pay attention to how you feel when you sing the words you've written. If you feel a little uncomfortable, maybe a tiny bit embarrassed even, you're on the right track. That's the dilemma everyone finds themselves in. There are only so many things anyone can say. So at some point, your focus will have to shift away from being concerned about "themes" and "meaning" and "what a song is about."

If you're doubting my assertion that it's more important to write with an authentic voice than it is to write with an interesting topic in mind, I'd challenge you to write something that means nothing to you at all. It may be harder than you think. I find it's almost impossible to put two words together and not find at least some meaning. We're conditioned to look for patterns and identify mysteries to solve much more than we are designed to dictate what we're searching for. I recommend allowing that natural curiosity and our sense-making brains to do their thing.

Let's try it. I just glanced at an open page in a book I was reading and the words "syrup" and "revival" entered my consciousness without any intention on my part. Syrup Revival!

Aside from their worthiness as a potential band name, I'd say I could come up with about a dozen reasons for these words to go into business together without breaking a sweat.

> *Come on down*
> *To the syrup revival*
> *It's sickening*
> *And sweet*
> *It's going to get you off your seat*
> *Up unto your feet*
> *The gospel's going to stick*
> *Once and for all*
> *At the syrup revival*

"Muzzle of Bees" is a phrase that formed out of some random association like this. It's weird to me now because I have such a clear image of what those words mean to me that I have to remind myself that I'm 90 percent sure I made it up and that it's not something that really existed before I wrote that song.

I Don't Have Musical Training
— or I Don't Know How to Play an Instrument —

So you want to write a song but you say to yourself, "I don't know anything about music." I could have said something like that about myself. I definitely don't have a background in music theory, and I don't read music. But I'm pretty confident in my ability to communicate music in my own way. To the person who says they don't know anything about music, I'd say, "Have you ever heard a song and responded to it? OK, you know music!" It's like saying that if you're not confident in your understanding of grammar, then you can't talk or write a word. Do you judge a painting based on how accurately the artist could name all of the colors on their palette? Of course not. It's ridiculous.

Maybe you feel reluctant to try writing a song because you don't play an instrument. That's a bigger challenge. But do you aspire to play an instrument? Do you have a computer? If you don't play an instrument or have a computer, no big deal. Do you have a a tape recorder, or a phone that can record voice memos? Do you have an actual voice? None of the above? Let's expand our definition of what a "song" is. If a song is memory in some way, let's create a moment that you won't forget. There are lots of ways to do that—let's see if we can figure out some. Can you fill your house with balloons before your wife gets home? That might be a little too much in Gwyneth Paltrow's Goop territory, but is there something else that you do that you can call a song? How about the way that you answer the phone when somebody calls you? Is that your signature? Is that a song? I like the idea of giving ourselves permission to knock down a lot of intellectual barriers and rhetorical cages when we think about songwriting.

That's why I feel so confident in telling other people that they can write a song. Because to a great extent, writing a song is really just the ability to hear it. To hear something that happened and to claim it as yours. Even things that are technically mistakes—wrong chords, missed beats, skewed harmonies . . . And that's another place people get mystical about it. It would be weirder if you never made sounds that were at least somewhat pleasing to you. Watch a little kid pluck a guitar for the first time—within minutes they start enjoying the sounds they're making with no instruction. They easily begin to create something fun and exciting. They'll entertain themselves. Now, I know that some instruments are prohibitively hard to get into, like some reeds—making a pleasing sound with them right off the bat is almost out of the question. But with a piano or a guitar, if you allow yourself the time and willingness to experiment, you will hear something that you want to keep. Or hear something that reminds you of something else. Songwriters are just people who have claimed those things—who give themselves credit. Who say they invented rock and roll. And you can do it, too. You just invented a song. You just invented music.

— I Don't Think I Have Enough Talent —

We all have certain gifts, but if we start comparing our gifts with other people's, we're always going to find someone who has more enviable traits. That's hard for humans not to do—to compare themselves with and measure themselves against someone else. And it can be very daunting and upsetting when people realize that others are more talented than they are. But you have to work through that. You can't quit because there's a Beyoncé in the world. You can't quit because you went to see the Chicago Symphony Orchestra and realized that everyone on stage knows more about music than you ever will.

There's always a blurry line between aptitude and gift. Someone might have a certain aptitude, and they might train themselves to be a practitioner of something. And others might have an artistic gift. And I look at the artistic gift as more about communication and the ability to be oneself. And not just about being able to execute a piece of music perfectly. To me, showing up with a reliably open heart and a will to share whatever spirit you can muster is what resonates and transcends technical perfection.

4

Make Songwriting a Habit

Be on the Side of Creation

OK, I hope I've disabused you of some notions about why you CAN'T be a songwriter. And I hope I've also convinced you that you really can do this, especially if you're truly willing to make songwriting a part of your life. Which brings me to the value of repetition and routine as a central part of any artistic process. This happens to be something I feel very confident in saying I'm great at. As I've said, and emphasized, earlier in the book, inspiration doesn't just happen—it has to be invited in, time and time again, through regular, concentrated work. I can get up and go to work writing songs with the best songwriters who have ever lived! I feel lucky to love it as much as I do. If your goal is to write songs and have it end up being your day job, there's really no substitute for a work ethic. Being able to organize my life around this primary goal has made me feel extremely fortunate. I have a place—Wilco's Loft, a combination practice space and recording studio in Chicago, a couple of miles from my house—where I get to go to write and record every day. I try not to take it for granted that I'll always have that, so I've tried to stay in touch with the daily habits of writing that don't require that luxury. For example, doing a bit of freewriting every morning—often before I even roll out of bed—something I'll talk about in more detail later in the book.

When I think about the evolution of my own process in writing songs, I believe I'm better than I used to be about adapting to whatever environment I'm in. I used to need it to be very simplified, to an almost pathological degree, especially when I was writing lyrics. I'd need things to be symmetrical or organized on my desk. It seemed like the way to organize my mind was to have a controlled space, to make sure what was in my field of vision was orderly-looking. Not as much with writing music as with writing lyrics, which seems to require a specific mind-set. I've learned to be more flexible about that now.

But I'm getting ahead of myself. We're still talking about you! I think a great way for anyone to get started is to develop a routine, to develop a structure that you want to form as a habit. It's much easier if you say, "I'm going to write songs for half an hour before I go to work in the morning," or "I'll do it as soon as I get home—and I'm going to reward myself with dinner, or a beer, once I've spent half an hour writing songs." I think using a notebook or a pad of paper or a voice-memo recorder, which most people have on their phones, is a habit you might as well start now. I know many successful songwriters have that habit. I definitely do. Don't take for granted that your ideas are so great that you'll remember them. I write down or put into my phone everything that ever crosses my mind that I think has potential, that twists my ear a little bit. I even record sounds I hear walking around outside that remind me of something musical. I just think, "I want to hear that again," and I don't know exactly why.

When I go back and listen to my voice memos, I'll hear a lot of snippets of songs on an acoustic guitar. And then there will be some strange birdsongs from Australia, and they'll both feel like me. I recorded birds, but I made a conscious decision to record that. I invented that. The act of doing that seems as creative to me as the act of playing something on a guitar. It reconfirms my search for beauty and inspiration. I forget about things I've done like that, and then they surprise me, and sometimes they become songs.

It's Hard Work but Shouldn't Be a Struggle

Some artists struggle. There is no disputing that. But I also think that a great fraud has been perpetrated on people because of how often that story gets told versus how

often the art happens without that external struggle—
and even more often, in spite of the artist's personal challenges. I guess it's easier to write about an artist if you
project a little magic onto the process. Art is difficult to
write about. And the more difficult the art is to comprehend, the harder it gets to share our impressions in coherent and illuminating ways. That's at least part of the
reason the artist becomes the story rather than the art.
And it's a pretty dull story to tell unless you have some
mental illness, drug addiction, deprivation, or depravity.
So the countless well-adjusted artists who just put their
heads down and work all the time don't tend to get written about quite as much without some type of hardship
being highlighted. And it's possible that the art of the
torment-free creation gets viewed with some degree of
skepticism, simply because the story about its creation is
less compelling.

That was a big hurdle for me, getting healthy—I
wrote about it a lot in my first book. However much I
disdained the notion of a drug-addled rock star, some
part of me still believed that creation myth, that you
have to suffer. And then I realized that everyone suffers.
Therefore, anyone who creates art can, if they choose,
focus on their suffering and say that's where it comes
from.

Does everyone suffer to the same degree? Probably
not. But we only understand our own suffering through
our own eyes. So I think the fact that everyone suffers is

enough. If it were only great suffering that created great art, I'd think there would be a lot more of it, sadly. I would also argue that it's pretty rare that someone who's truly debilitated is able to create at all. Not to mention how much art isn't being made by the artists we've lost to illnesses and sorrows.

For me, and for most songwriters I know, writing songs is hard work. I don't think that hard work is a struggle, though. That's the difference. Working hard is a noble pursuit. I don't know what else there is besides work. I talk about that a bit in my first book, too—that there was this notion that being in a rock band was a good thing to do if you didn't want to work or get a real job. But all the rock bands you've heard of are the rock bands that've worked the hardest. I get that there are some areas of the music business where some bands were shafted, and there wasn't a uniform fairness to paying off the people who worked the hardest. But it's probably pretty unlikely that you've heard of the people who didn't work at all. Whenever I see someone like Beyoncé, I think, "She's working harder than anyone on earth."

I do think there's a lot of soul-crushing work, and a lot of unfortunate circumstances where people are tied to something they can't get out of because it's the only way to sustain their family's existence. But that's all inspiration to work harder at what you do love doing, in my opinion. Because if you get to do something you love, you're part of a small minority of the billions of humans who have ever walked the earth. That says to me that you should cherish it, and protect it, and do everything you can to ensure that it's not corrupted, that it's not taken from you and made into something less fulfilling. Protect your inspiration, protect your ability to be inspired.

5

Everyday Work
Regular Practice

I've been trying to push you toward a daily work ethic, so at this point I'm going to share mine in detail. In the next part of the book, I'll share specific exercises that will benefit you through repeated use and regular practice. This might sound overstructured to some people, but personally I love working this way. I love the routine and how it allows me to disappear from the process just enough to be surprised by something I've written. And I trust that if I'm paying attention, things that just happen with seeming randomness are almost always more interesting than the ideas I start out with.

Here are the three main items I have on a daily mental checklist. I'll note that these are all tools I use to write many songs over time, but they'll work just as well if your purpose is to write just one song.

1. **Stockpiling Words, Language, and Lyrics**—doing exercises like freewriting, writing poems, refining, and revising, all of which I'll talk about in the next section

2. **Stockpiling Music, Songs, and Parts of Songs**—making demo recordings, practicing, learning other people's songs, and writing parts for songs in progress

3. **Pairing Words and Music**—writing lyrics to a melody and searching for matches between stockpiled demos and lyric sets, poems, and freewriting

On most days I manage to get all three checked off to some degree without much of a struggle. But I feel generally satisfied and that I've maintained my work ethic even when I'm able to knock only one off the list. It doesn't take much: If you keep it up for any length of time, you are going to accumulate a lot of material for songs, even if you're able to set aside only five to ten minutes a day.

Here's an overview of an ideally productive day of writing. You may note an absence of "family time" or any other types of normal activity. While I do condone "family time," the sad truth is that "family time" is really "not-gonna-happen time" when it comes to my output, and the time I spend with my loving family produces very little in terms of pure songwriting material. Feel free to have a life. But don't complain to me when it takes you a month to finish your first song. I'm kidding here. This "schedule" is really meant to be an idealized outline of what a perfect day of uninterrupted creative time might look like. I'm not sure I've *ever* really checked all of these boxes in one twenty-four-hour period. I probably have but I'm nuts for this stuff. Point is, your family is obviously way more important than anything else. And contrary to what I just said, spending time with your family is living your life, which is way better than writing about your life. Also, it gives you something to write about. If you want to be a songwriter, you're going to have to find a balance. The picture this day planner paints is what I might do with an entire empty day after having vigorously lived my life enough to earn it.

8 p.m.–10 p.m.

OK. I know this isn't when a lot of people would start their day, but stick with me here. This is the time of day when I like to listen through some voice memos of simple guitar ideas or chord progressions and hummed melodies that I've documented on my phone until I find something interesting to play around with. Sometimes it can take me a while to relearn my own songs, but I've gotten better over the years at keeping a record of the

tunings I'm playing in and/or capo positions. But there
are some songs from long ago that I've never been able to
figure out. Songs that will never be finished . . . sigh.
Not because I was playing like Segovia that day and it's
just too advanced to relearn, but because I was a lazy
idiot and didn't bother to write down the crazy cool tuning I invented. Lesson learned.

Once I get a handle on how to play something, I'll
play it over and over until I start to get a sense of a general shape it might want to take as a completed song. But
what I mostly want at this early stage is a good strong
verse and an equally strong chorus. Bridges—those short
musical sections that "bridge" other more substantive
sections of songs—often serve as a respite before diving
back into the main repeated melody of a song. Sometimes they're called middle-eights. You know what they
are even if you didn't know what they were called. Think
the "When I'm home . . ." part in "A Hard Day's Night."
Now while the melody is fresh in my mind, I'll start
looking for some lyrical ideas that feel right for the tune,
either by scanning through my stockpiled lyrics and
poems or by doing one of the melody-oriented exercises
in Part III. This is one of the most exciting and fulfilling stages of a song's creation. I'm always amazed when
something jumps off the page and marries itself to
the melody. Every time it happens, it feels like a minor
miracle.

10 p.m.–12 a.m.

Take a break. Spend some time with the family. Do my crossword puzzle. (Yes, I'm a crossword puzzle nerd/ addict, but it sure beats the hell out of when I was an *addict* addict.)

12 a.m.–? (often 3 a.m.–ish)

I usually take this time right before I go to sleep to focus on getting lyrics set in place enough to sing at least one verse and one chorus into my phone. If I'm really making progress, I might write a half dozen or so verses while I have the meter/cadence and rhyme scheme locked in.

Why do I do this? Because I believe that you need to put yourself, consciously, in the path of your subconscious. To trust yourself that there are things you can get to. But your ego is working against you; it doesn't trust your subconscious to come up with anything near as smart as you are.

We carry around a lot of stuff we don't always know how to get to, but it's there. Drugs and alcohol are looked at as being good for writing and good for creativity because they do seem to relax our inhibitions about getting to our subconscious and also about getting back. Personally speaking, I often worried after I stopped doing drugs that the association I had with my subconscious was related to my use, and that going there sober would trigger some desire to use. Sometimes I would even get scared about never being able to get back to my rational mind if I fully gave myself over to dreaming up songs without an observing ego calling all the shots. Having just made peace with an inner voice that I was still learning how to use in my effort to stay sober, I found that letting go of my ego turned out to be more disorienting than it had been in the past. It turns out those concerns were completely unwarranted. Drugs can help expand your consciousness, and they do allow for some exploration of the deeper layers of connections and associations we all have with the world. But a blowtorch can light a cigarette, too, and in order to get to your subconscious, I'd recommend using something a little more reasonable and, dare I say, safer.

However, the good news is that you really can develop skills, habits, and activities that will calm your mind and let things pour out of you more easily. Walking tends to unravel the knots in my thinking, and I'll always recommend a leisurely stroll or even a brisk one around the block to alleviate almost any kind of mental stress. Whether it's related to feeling stuck on a song or trapped in life, it's an easy "next right thing to do" when you need something to help simplify your thoughts. This is just some general advice, not necessarily recommended for this particular time of day. In fact, I would like to actively discourage you from taking a walk during the small hours of the morning. I'm not sure how this bit of advice ended up in this section. In summary:

Walks = good. Walks in the dead of night = I urge caution.

What is ideal for this time slot is working on songs to have them in your head right before you go to bed, and then again first thing in the morning when you wake up. I truly think I do a lot of my best work while I'm asleep. I often wake up with the last musical puzzle I was contemplating completely solved. No joke! Try it! I've even had nearly complete sets of all new lyrics settle themselves down on the last melody I was singing before I fell asleep.

Sometimes even before getting out of bed in the morning, I write down lyrics on my phone almost as if I were taking dictation from my half-asleep, kinder, temporarily less judgmental brain. Sleeping can really untangle your most troublesome thoughts. You just have to get good at falling asleep when your mind is still a little active and engaged. Which might be a problem for some people, I'll admit. Fortunately for me, sleeping has always been an area in which I excel. I've always been able to flip a switch, so to speak, when my head hits the pillow. In fact, it drives my wife nuts how easily I can go from conversing with her to a corpselike deep sleep. Maybe you're not as lucky, but there must be a time between shutting down active thought and activity and relaxing for the evening—find whatever your version of that is. Just try to focus on your song with some intent in whatever moments you have before you zone out. Also, this same trick works extremely well for learning difficult passages of music. I'll often practice a guitar part I'm struggling with right before bed, and it's almost magical how much easier it is to play the next morning.

7 a.m.–9 a.m.

This is the part that gets a bit mystical. But it happens so reliably that I trust it's something I've stumbled upon that has at least some scientific basis. I consider the ease with which writing flows out of me in the morning—both writing I've been working on the night before and brand-new lyrics and music—as a part of the process that has some natural, if not divine (if that's the right word) reason for working so well at that particular time. Of course, all that comes with the same caveat as any other step in the songwriting process: It's not always great. It's not like I'm promising this method is guaranteed to turn every lyricist into Leonard Cohen. But I love how much freer my associations become when I combine my semi-sleep state with the rhythms and melodies that have been danced to in my dreams all night long.

9 a.m.–11 a.m.

Nap. Right, I know I'm in an incredibly unique position, and not everyone is going to convert to some polyphasic sleep schedule just because I recommended it in service of songwriting. But here we are, and I'm just trying to be honest about what my ideal writing day could look like. Also, I am a big advocate of napping in general. But you have to remember I've been in a touring rock band with a full crew and buses for a majority of my time on earth, and the reality of that lifestyle is that you only really need to be awake around three hours out of every twenty-four, and even that can be optional depending on how many shows you've done in a row.

11 a.m.–12 p.m.

I usually use this period of time to either do some free-writing, maybe some word exercise, or to look at what I wrote when I was up at 7 a.m. Or if there's a song I'm planning on working on that day in the studio, I'll try to make sure it's in a shape close enough to a final form to start recording.

12 p.m.–6 p.m.

I typically spend this time in the studio. Again, I realize this is a luxury, and I wouldn't want anyone to assume I take it for granted. My lifelong dream has always been to have someplace to go where I could surround myself with musical equipment and immerse myself in the making of music anytime I feel moved to do so, day or night. Over the years, almost all my energy and resources have gone into building this dream scenario, and now I spend almost as much energy maintaining it. I get that if it weren't for some crazy cosmic fluke, it would simply not be feasible to have the Loft, which has helped me be so productive over the years. But everyone needs a space to work, and while yours might not look like mine, finding an environment that makes you feel good and puts your mind in an open and receptive state is definitely one of the most important things you can do for yourself as any type of creator.

6 p.m.–8 p.m.

I know I don't look like I'm in tip-top physical shape, but I kind of am. My cardio condition is actually kind of great. I ran for years until my addictive nature resulted in two fractured shins. For a while I was committed to swimming daily, but that turned out to be a colossal hassle on the road. Stationary biking ended up being the ticket. Thanks for asking. I'm not bragging for no reason, by the way. It's all a part of the bigger picture to me. Exercise is essential to my mental health, and it absolutely has been an essential part of my creative regimen. Not to mention how much it's helped me as a singer. At the very least, taking regular long walks is a well-known and reliable rejuvenating habit writers of all types have sworn by for probably as long as being a writer has been something one can be. It must have something to do with getting your body involved and out of the way of your mind. Physical movement, I would imagine, also makes it difficult to maintain any sense of being stuck psychologically. So yeah. Go for walks. If you want to write a song, take a walk.

6

What You Get in the End
Process Versus Goals

Finally, now that we've discussed the rest—why you want to write a song, what's keeping you from writing a song—and started to talk about process and why it's good to have a daily routine, let's address this notion of an end goal. What is it exactly that you would like to accomplish? If you bought this book, I'm guessing you already know what your number one goal is: to write one song, and after that, ideally, more songs.

But let's just go ahead and remind ourselves that while it is important to aim at things we'd like to achieve, I truly believe, with songwriting, that being in the "process" has to at least be *a* goal if not the only goal. For me personally, the writing itself has definitely become the primary goal. Being fully engaged with a song I'm working on is what I look forward to the most in my life.

Yes, I still have goals and desires. I want to finish

albums and be able to provide myself with new songs to perform, but the feeling I get when I write—the sense that time is simultaneously expanding and disappearing, that I'm simultaneously more me and also free of me—is the main reason I wanted to put my thoughts on songwriting down in book form to share with everyone so inclined. It has to be the going and not just the getting there when it comes to songwriting, or any artistic endeavor, really. And I'd like to focus on that and share more of what I think is the only truly shareable part of making songs—what songwriting itself achieves, rather than just what a finished song achieves. Although I wouldn't be surprised if you end up with both.

— It's OK to Fail —

Finished songs aren't often going to be what you hoped they would be. You're going to fail. A lot. In the end, learning how to write songs is, in large part, about teaching yourself to fail and being OK with it. But it's also about searching for, finding, and sharing some truth. That's what I'm looking for in everybody's music, in every genre—having the truth exposed. A truth always comes out in art. I think comedy finds it, and I think good songwriting finds it. I believe that all art is about this truth, which is almost invisible at most other times, when we're less aware, locked in the drudgery of our day-to-day existences, until art breaks through and points it out to us.

Sometimes I think of it as a search for low-hanging fruit, even though I know that's not quite the right simile—it's something people walk by all the time, something so ingrained in our environment that it's become invisible, something so obvious nobody sees it anymore, but then someone figures out how to say what it is, or how to see it, and everyone else says, "Of course! Why didn't I say that? That's exactly right. I always knew that was there," or "That's exactly how I feel." Like when Bill Callahan sings, "Well, I can tell you about the river / Or we could just get in."

And as much as I say you need to be willing and eager to fail, I also think it's OK to want to be great. I don't feel any shame in saying I want to write the greatest song in the world. I want to write a song that would make someone say, "This is my favorite song of all time." People often say that and mean it in the moment, but I want them to say it and mean it about my song.

That being said, most of my time spent creating is not actively in pursuit of writing the greatest song in the world. I'm more focused on just being very satisfied with the idea that I'm not hurting anybody. It's a process, and whatever happens, that's great. I come out of my creative state at some point to look through what I've created and find enough pieces that make me think, "That's really good. I should share that." But all the time spent creating, if I'm in the right frame of mind, is not really so much about "Is this good or bad?" There's just a lot of joy in it, in having created something at all. I don't feel as bad about other things. I don't necessarily feel high, or *overly* joyed. I just feel like, "Oh, I'm not wasting my time."

— **What Do You Get Out of It?** —

So let's suppose for a second you just wrote a song. Seconds ago. You just put down the guitar. What can you expect to get out of it? This is an incredibly rich question for anyone with a bent for philosophizing. Part of me wants to say, "Not much," and another says, "Everything!" I hold both these opinions with equal strength. But they're not exactly answering the same question, are they? In the first case, I would say, "Not much," because this book's basic premise is to help you find a process and an inclination to be absorbed into that process enough to have it reliably result in a song—that is, after you've finished that first one, of course. I'd call this the "going," not the "getting there." What you make of the song or what the world will make of it is of little concern when contrasted with the joy that I've talked about many times now—the joy of disappearing long enough to find something you didn't know you had inside you.

I truly believe that. For me, it's a thing I do that has become such a habit, and has so consistently comforted me in a private way, that I have to stop myself from time to time. Otherwise I would never take the final necessary steps—arranging and recording—needed to dress my songs up enough to send them out into the world. I'd just have hundreds of half-naked song babies all wanting attention. But every once in a while, a song is "everything," and I want you to have that, too. Every once in a while, you luck out and you get at something no other art form can touch. It's mostly in the melody, I think, but it really could be any element of a song that clicks into its slot just so. And the song becomes a place. Where it truly is everything. Its own universe. The only place you can go to feel the way that song makes you feel. I can't say it happens a lot, and I can't guarantee you'll ever get there, but it's too great a feeling to pretend it isn't something you can dream about. Maybe you can create a place that makes someone feel like they're floating weightless inside a small guitar the way Nick Drake's "Pink Moon" makes me feel, or maybe you can map some uncharted region the way Missy Elliott does with "Get Ur Freak On."

Of course, I would be lying if I didn't also mention a part of me that wants acknowledgment. That wants to be a "legend" or wants to be respected and revered for what it is that I do. I imagine everybody feels like that a little bit. I think it's pretty natural.

Personally, I've had the good fortune of having overshot whatever existed in my mind's eye of what I thought it would look like to be famous during the first year I made records. The people I pictured were riding around in vans, playing in punk rock clubs. Suddenly I was thinking, "Oh, I guess we're playing theaters now." Then it became a fun challenge. Do I belong here? Can I get good enough to be on this stage without embarrassing myself? I really believe—and this is where it gets sort of touchy-feely—that if you're sincerely bringing yourself out of yourself by making music, and you're getting so much out of it yourself, and *then* the world starts to hear what you're doing and they respond to it . . . I can't help feeling that's the best way to exploit your gift, by letting the work come first.

But that doesn't mean that you shouldn't want recognition, and I admit, I want it, too. Look, I know that a lot of people in this world have no idea who I am. And if I were really obsessed with that notion, I could probably do things to get that kind of fame, but I would be less happy, I think. Once that becomes the primary focus, so many things become more important than the music, and it never ends. It's like rich people with yachts—once you have the biggest yacht ever built up to that point, someone is going to get a bigger yacht.

I'm not trying to write a self-help book, but here's what I'm getting at: In writing songs, I have found something that overwhelmingly makes me a happier person, more able to cope with the world. Can this be transferred to anybody, regardless of talent level, regardless of their individual gift for creativity? I absolutely think it can, and I hope I've already convinced you.

⸺ Do It for Love ⸺

That is what I want to convey, more than anything, before we move on to the actual mechanics of writing a song. But you have to stop thinking that you're going to make something great, or something that might make you famous. You have to stop thinking about anything other than what happened when you were a little kid, and you laid on the floor, and you drew. And you lost yourself in that drawing. And in the end, you absolutely loved that drawing because you made it yourself. And the drawing got hung up on the fridge regardless of how good it was, because your mom loves you and everybody loves you. Why can't you be that kind to yourself?

Or maybe your mom didn't like your drawing and told you so. People are going to judge you at some point, and you're definitely going to judge yourself. But it's still so worth it—putting the crayon in your hand, putting the pen in your hand, putting the guitar in your hand. There's so much value to that, and it's so much more valuable than any criticism that's going to come your way.

That's one of the problems with humans—that we can be talked out of loving something. That we can be talked out of loving something that we do, and we can be talked out of loving ourselves. Easily, unfortunately. Sometimes parents, because they're afraid the world is going to do it, would rather prepare their children in their own way for how much the world doesn't care, doesn't love them. Or doesn't love what they do. It's wrong. Maybe the world is going to do that, maybe it won't. But you shouldn't do that to your kids.

I guess you could look at everyone as being a kid, but not everybody is in touch with it. And maybe some of that has to do with some dysfunction, some kind of trauma at a certain age that tamps down a certain amount of emotional growth and keeps you touching back on this particular part of your life as the part that's the most sustaining.

I think one of the issues that we're talking about is this idea that gifts are rare, that not everybody has gifts. I don't know if that's true. I'd like to believe that it's not true. I'd like to believe that everybody, if allowed to pursue their dreams and passions, would have a gift for something. A gift for making somebody feel better, maybe. It just seems like humans . . . we've got to all be good at something.

I was a late bloomer in a lot of ways. I wasn't a virtuoso guitar player. I wasn't a great singer. I wasn't good in school, because I wasn't focused. But I was obsessed with music. I'm so grateful that I was able to hold on to that childlike passion that I had for music. I love that I feel that way. I love that I feel like I still need to get better at this. But I am good at this, and I feel good that I get to do it.

But I know I'm lucky—it's not hard for me anymore, and I don't worry about it the way I used to. I sit down, and I just know that something's going to come out, and it's not going to hurt anybody. And most of the time, I'm going to think, "Holy shit! Where did that come from?" But I know where it came from, and I know that it's still me. I have a shameful amount of gratitude. It's hard to express sometimes, because I think it might turn people off, the overwhelming gratitude I feel for it all. And that, exactly, is what I want to share with you, and how I hope you'll feel after you're done reading this book and writing your song.

PART II

7

Start Writing

The Music of Words

OK, time to really get started on your one song, the one song we've been talking about, theoretically, for almost seventy pages. In this part, and in this chapter, you're actually going to start writing it.

Remember the three things I do every day when I'm writing songs? We're going to address each, in order—not that you have to do anything in a particular order, or that songwriting is always linear. But let's start writing in a linear fashion by focusing our attention on the music of words and creating at least fragments of lyrics that have a basic connection to melodies.

Why words? Because I believe all words have their own music. And along with that music, I believe words contain worlds of words and meanings that are, more often than not, locked beneath the surface. Poetry is what happens when words are opened up, and those worlds within are made visible, and the music behind the words is heard. And songs do that, too, just in a different order.

Songs and poems exist for very similar reasons, in my mind. I think they were probably one and the same for a long period of human existence, to remember history and important events, and remember people, too. I believe that poetry came into existence because people needed it—if it were easy to write down and record things without poetry, we wouldn't have needed poetry. But for some reason we did. And I think it's at least partially because we lacked the proper devices to record things in those times, and also because we understood the fallibility of our memories, that we made tonal mnemonics. Some languages evolved to be tonal, even. How often do you still sing the ABCs to yourself when you're asked to alphabetize something? No shame! I can never remember my own lyrics without singing them out loud, and even then I struggle without a guitar in my hands to steer me into the melodic lanes of my memory.

I'm not a linguist, I'm not super versed in all that. But it makes sense to me that words would retain some primordial kernel of music. Sometimes it's clearer by putting one word next to another, but I think the music inside words exists to some degree whether we listen for it or not. Which gets us to our starting point. Let's start training our ear to listen to words as the basic building blocks of songs.

— Which Comes First? —

When you write songs, the one question you get asked more than any other is "Which comes first, music or lyrics?" Starting here—with words being sounds and music, but not necessarily thinking about meaning just yet—is the best way I can think of to emphasize that the answer I often give to that question, "Both and neither," isn't meant to be evasive or condescending. It's really how I try to approach the creation of my songs. It's a process I love. So in this part, let's take a look at some of the tricks and exercises I use to let my ego-driven, meaning-obsessed brain off the hook for a while; let's allow words to be musical and atomic; and let's start moving them around a little bit. Hopefully these exercises and tricks can help make words alone be musical enough to hear something you didn't expect, or make you see a word in a new/unexpected way. And I think all of that is songwriting, all of that is poetry. And all of that is related to what we're here to do, and talk about, and create.

— Hot-Wiring Language —

I look at all these exercises as a way to hot-wire language, to start it up again. Another analogy would be to think of these as detours around your linguistic habits. It can become difficult to hear music in the way we talk, because we all tend to focus on a certain style of communicating. I think all the exercises below are a very helpful way to limber up our use of language, to soften up our brains so that words can make more of an impression on them. Our thinking and the way we communicate can be very rigid, and words just bounce off the surface tension of our overtaxed attention. This is all fine and natural for our day-to-day communication needs. But in order to write songs, most of us direct some intention into the mix to free language from those needs and allow it to reveal beauty and pain, or whatever else is hiding beneath the outer layers of everyday language.

You want words to burst into the room, demand your attention, and remind you how exciting things can be. You have a responsibility to challenge yourself to use them in a way that is more vivid than your normal daily usage.

— Keep the Language Simple —

That being said, I think it's important to make the point that I'm not talking about expanding your vocabulary. I mean, that's always a nice thing to do in the name of self-improvement. But fancy multisyllabic words aren't going to make a lyric better, and are very often the type of thing that breaks the spell being cast by a melody when I listen to music. Like, "How long has this guy been trying to shoehorn 'plethora' into a tune?!" In fact, I would say that most of my favorite songwriters consciously stick to common, simple, and precise language, but they don't use it in a common and simple way within a song or melody. I'm thinking of people like John Prine, who didn't use a lot of big words or flowery language. But when he did, I believe he always stayed true to the song and what needed to be said, over any desire to make himself sound smart or poetic.

So to paraphrase that Bill Callahan lyric I quoted earlier, we can keep talking about the river or we could just get in. There isn't anything to be afraid of. Have I stressed that enough? The worst that can ever happen when we spend time with ourselves being creative is so low-stakes, I can hardly come up with an example other than the mild frustrations we've already identified as stumbling blocks. The rewards, however, are limitless, and you don't have to take my word for it. We have thousands of years of evidence that songs help us live and cope, and they teach us how to be human. Becoming a part of the continuation of that rich human activity is all up to you. An endless flowing river of song. And you get to add your voice. No one ever drowns. Dive in.

8

EXERCISE 1:

Word Ladder— Verbs and Nouns

As I've said, the exercises I'm suggesting are all aimed at loosening up the habitual way we use language and the shortcuts we all take by rote when we converse and communicate at our most basic level all day long, and then taking those new ways to think about language and turning them into the beginnings of lyrics, into the beginnings of songs.

One of the ways we narrow our daily language is by creating more expected, more manageable pairings of words in our speech patterns. For example, we tend to use the same verbs with the same nouns. We tend to use the same adjectives to emphasize the same nouns. Here's an example of a noun and a noun pair that drives me nuts: "smattering of applause." You don't ever hear someone say "a smattering of . . ." anything else. But a "smattering of teeth" or a "smattering of heartbeats" are both wildly evocative pairings that immediately form images in my mind.

At a more basic level, avoiding adverbs and adjectives is just good all-around writing advice. You don't need to tell anyone "the dog barked loudly." Because adding "loudly" to that sentence actually makes the word "bark" quiet. Some of us repeat the same phrases to the point where our closest friends and family can often finish our sentences or even predict what we're about to say. I think we all do this to some degree because it makes communication more efficient. It's much more important to be understood when asking "Where is the fire extinguisher?" than it is to invent a beautiful and inspiring sentence: "Tell me, won't you, how I may put my hand to the shiny red savior of our soon-to-be-ablaze breakfast nook?" Clichés can be helpful, sometimes even necessary. You might eventually be able to use them as larger building blocks of songs, which can be enlivened and twisted into more interesting shapes by placing them in fresher contexts or even through repetition.

But we're getting ahead of ourselves. Let's start with a few basic ingredients and see if we can make something exciting happen. An example to start . . .

Come up with ten verbs that are associated with, say, a physician, and write them down on a page. Then write down ten nouns that are within your field of vision.

Examine   Cushion
Thump   Guitar
Prescribe   Wall
Listen   Turntable
Write   Sunlight
Scan   Window
Touch   Carpet
Wait   Drum
Charge   Microphone
Heal   Lightbulb

Now take a pencil and draw lines to connect nouns and verbs that don't normally work together. I like to use this exercise not so much to generate a set of lyrics but to remind myself of how much fun I can have with words when I'm not concerning myself with meaning or judging my poetic abilities. Here's an example of a quick poem I might make trying to use all of the words above.

> *the drum is waiting*
> *by the window listening*
> *where the sunlight writes*
> *on the cushions*
> *prescribed*
> *thump the microphone*
> *the guitar is healing*
> *how the turntable is touched*
> *charging the wall*

> *while one lightbulb examines*
> *and scans the carpet*

OK. It isn't the greatest poem ever written. But I bet it's not the worst. It might be difficult to sing, and it might not make quite enough sense to follow, but already I'm loving the way some of the scenes are being drawn—the phrase "sunlight writes" makes me think of a hidden world, full of mystery and clues, and alludes to an idea that the natural world might have intentions, might be trying to tell us something . . . Anyway, that's the exercise, and I find it almost always works when I'm feeling a need to break out of my normal, well-worn paths of language.

While we're here, I might as well show you how I'd try to make the exercise into something more songlike. I can relax all the rules we just followed for now, and hopefully something that makes more sense will emerge. For this poem/lyric I can use whatever I want from the first-draft poem, but I'm not obligated to use every word from the original list. I'm not going to even hold myself to the nouns being nouns and the verbs being verbs.

> *the drum is waiting by the windowsill*
> *where the sunlight writes its will on the rug*
> *my guitar is healed*
> *by the amp plug charging the wall*

and that's not all
I'm always in love

There. That's still a bit awkward, but it's definitely enough to jump-start my brain in a way where language and words have my full attention again. Which is the right mind-set to be in when you're creating lyrics, or at least fragments of lyrics.

You may have noticed the last line is familiar. I thought I'd take advantage of this exercise to illustrate how much easier it is to write with a melody in mind. So instead of coming up with new melody, I used the Wilco song "I'm Always in Love." Go ahead and sing that whole verse to yourself if you're familiar with that song. Now, I don't think it's an improvement, necessarily, but it gives you an idea of how it feels when you combine any of this type of thinking about words with a melodic idea to trace over. Which is kind of the basic idea of the next exercise.

9

EXERCISE 2:

Stealing Words from a Book

This exercise, which is similar to the first in terms of getting you started with lyric pieces and fragments, is a bit more free-form in its execution, but I swear it can be really helpful when you find yourself mining a tired vein of your normal vocabulary. Think of a melody, like I did with "I'm Always in Love" in the last chapter—it doesn't have to be your own for the sake of learning this process. Open up a book anywhere, any page, and keep humming the melody to yourself as you scan. Don't really try to comprehend what you're reading; just let your mind skim over the surface of the words on the page and focus your attention on the melody. If you can get in the right frame of mind, words will jump out and attach themselves to the melody. Highlight (literally, with a highlighter, if you can) those words, and keep moving until you've collected a cache of words that potentially sound right in the context of your melody. Again, this might take some trial and error before it becomes helpful. I like this exercise a lot because it puts my ego securely in the backseat, far away from the steering wheel, and forces me to surrender to a process that puts language/words in front of my creative path, and I'm free to find them as though they've come from somewhere else (because they have). So I feel more free to react with surprise and passion or cold indifference than I am able to when my intellect begins treating my lyrical ideas like precious jewels.

Sometimes it's easier once you have an anchor word that snaps it all into place. For example, you're scanning the page, and all of a sudden the word "catastrophe" matches itself to the cadence and movement of the notes you're humming—that's a beautiful word, by the way, one that has a lot of melodic movement in it. It has an internal rhyme—ca-ta-stro-phe. That's like a musical moment in itself. It's easy to find some single-syllable words to connect it together: "Wouldn't you call it a ca-tastrophe?"

But you don't have to get that deep into it yet. You might write down your anchor word, whatever it is, and maybe find a rhyming word, maybe get out a rhyming dictionary (or search "catastrophe + rhymes" online; it's really helpful) to find another word that might be exciting as part of a couplet. Before you know it, a story might start to emerge that has nothing to do with the source text. At which point this exercise has worked its magic, and you can follow what you've been given by the process to a satisfying conclusion. For instance,

> *wouldn't you call it a catastrophe*
> *when you realize you'd rather be*
> *anywhere but where you are*
> *and far from the one you want to see*

Or you can keep moving. Humming and scanning along until you've stockpiled more lyrical prompts or ideas than you'll ever need for your typical three- or four-verse song. I think it's important to stress that you should actually overdo it in terms of coming up with lyrics and words you like whenever you have the energy and time. Writing more than you need is almost never going to make a song worse. Sometimes every good line doesn't make it into the song you're working on. But that doesn't mean you have to throw those lines away.

I go back and look at the pages of lyrics I've written with this process—for instance, Henry Miller's line "Stand still like the hummingbird" was the inspiration behind one of the more requested Wilco songs—and find things I love, even ones I never used, frequently. It helps for there to be some length of time between when they were written and revisited, especially for it to be long enough for the initial melody to have faded. At this point, you're not committing yourself to anything. You're just creating building blocks.

Of course you CAN have an idea in your mind of what kind of song you want to write while you're doing these exercises. You're always free to do things however you want. But for this particular lyric-generating activity, nothing should be in the front of your mind as much as the melody.

I've been doing this for so long that most of my books have highlights all through them. People come over and pick up some book laying around and think, "He must have found this very interesting. I wonder what prompted him to study the Gnostic Gospels." Nope. Just liked the words.

10

EXERCISE 3:

Cut-Up Techniques

This is a good exercise to add to either of the previous two exercises, or possibly to shake up a set of lyrics that feel flat, lifeless, and rote. Basically, this technique requires some prewritten text. So grab something that you've been working on and write it all down on a legal pad. Or if you have access to a printer, print it out double-spaced. You can probably see where this is going. The cut-up technique requires scissors, or at the very least a steady tearing hand. The easiest cutting strategy is line by line, but word by word or phrase by phrase can provide equally interesting results.

Once you've cut up your text, you can either put the strips in a hat or turn them over and pull each line/word/phrase randomly. Then scan your randomly chosen poem construction for any unexpected surprises. I almost always find at least one newly formed phrase or word relationship that moves me or makes me smile. Another way to use your cut-up strips is to forget about trying to make random associations and just use them as movable modules of language. It's always fascinating to me how much more alive lines I've written can become when I'm able to have a simple tactile experience reorganizing the order and syntax of the lines and phrases.

I am aware I did not invent this technique. Nor am I the first to proselytize its usefulness in songwriting. And I know it might seem over the top, especially since I'm already asking you to shake up the language that you use. Also, some might think that this type of surrealist technique would be less applicable to the simpler and more direct styles of lyric writing. If that's the avenue you feel most drawn to, I feel duty-bound to implore you to give it a shot anyway. I can tell you that, for me, the songs that have been most transformed by implementing this method have almost always been the most traditional and direct.

For example, the lyrics to the song "An Empty Corner" initially were sung in this order:

> *In an empty corner of a dream*
> *My sleep could not complete*
> *Left on a copy machine*
> *Eight tiny lines of cocaine*

Sometimes just taking the last line in a verse and making it the opening lyric can reveal something more vivid and true that was being subdued by the line's former location. Or being overshadowed by the musical weight of needing to anchor the melody.

> *Eight tiny lines of cocaine*
> *Left on a copy machine*
> *In an empty corner of a dream*
> *My sleep could not complete*

This version is so much more powerful and better overall that I can't believe I ever tried to sing these lyrics in any other order. I'm tempted to make some convoluted analogy to the importance birth order can have on the dispositions of siblings, but I think I'll leave it at this: Take the time to play with your words. Allow yourself the joy of getting to know them without being precious about directing everything they are trying to say. It's still you! The decisions are still yours.

There are no accidents. Or at least there are no accidents that can't be embraced and claimed as what you meant to say all along. I honestly believe that making the decision to open yourself up to what might be within your work that isn't completely intentional is a brave act of acceptance and every bit as revealing and artful as any art that claims to be a fully realized vision.

11

EXERCISE 4:

Word Ladder Variation— the Dreaded Adjective

Another worthwhile variation to try involves revisiting the exercise we did with nouns and verbs. But in this word ladder, I'd like to try a simple variation so that I can illustrate how the same rote patterns of language can attach themselves to these word pairings and how liberating it can be to take adjectives, in particular, out of their usual environments and let them twist and contort nouns they've never been related to.

I'd also like to (again) make a brief statement of caution regarding adjectives and adverbs and how their overuse can create a flat and visually static type of lyric, which I think is best avoided. However, some people do get away with using a lot of adjectives. One of the things I've learned from observing Bob Dylan (versus people who try to write like Dylan) is that HE can break that rule and use as many adjectives as he wants, but personally, I feel I need to earn them.

Maybe that's a problem common to all types of creative writing, but adjective overuse can get out of hand if you don't watch out. Don't let adjectives make you think you're being poetic. An "impatient red fiery orb loomed in the whiskey-blurred, cottony-blue sky" is rarely going to hit me anywhere near as hard as "I was drunk in the day." Just saying. I don't think it's a wise choice for most people to head down that path. Of course, it's strange how adding words to paint a clearer, more specific image often muddies the image you're trying to expose. The problem is when they are used to spice up a vague verb or noun instead of replacing that with precise language. There are so many great words. Find them!

"I was extremely frightened by the very large man behind the counter" versus "I was petrified by the colossus working the register." OK? You get it. Just making sure. Anyway, I think it's pretty clear which sentence is more interesting and vivid.

So, back to adjectives and nouns (or adverbs and verbs if you prefer). Here's a list of ten adjectives related to outer space set against ten nouns that just popped into my head.

Circular	Ladder
Distant	Kiss
Ancient	Daughter

Haloed	Hand
Cold	Pool
Vast	Summer
Bright	Lawn
Frozen	Friend
Silent	Blaze
Infinite	Window

there is a distant hand
on a frozen ladder
climbing through
a bright window
a vast pool waiting
beside a silent lawn
where a daughter haloed
lives a circular summer
one cold kiss
from an infinite friend
away from an ancient blaze

Again, it's not a perfect poem, but it took me only about fifteen minutes to complete, and I really do enjoy some of the imagery that emerged. I actually found a few bits of language that I've been looking for to complete a song I've been working on. Even if you don't end up being a songwriter, I think sitting down from time to time to play with words in this manner can be oddly comforting. Whenever I do one of these exercises, I'm reminded how much beauty we have at our fingertips and how creating doesn't always mean that you have to cast yourself as the creator. In these cases I feel more like I'm participating in an activity that reveals my creative nature, that uncovers the hidden desire for there to be more meaning—the powerful longing I have for things to exist that I wasn't aware of. Or even the beauty that I witnessed being born.

12

EXERCISE 5:

Have a Conversation

Let's say you've gone through the previous exercises and you're still skeptical about the notion that any type of word game is going to help you write the types of song you feel you want to write. Or maybe you're just generally suspicious of your ability to make things up. Possibly, you're still convinced that you have nothing to say or even that you have to have something to say to write a song. I hear you. Songs have overweighted importance in our lives for all sorts of reasons. But I'm here to convince you that you are a born composer and improviser of language. And while most things that can be said have been said in song already, you have something to add to that conversation, just through each individual way of saying what's important to you, even if it isn't wholly (or even partly) original.

Which brings us to the concept of conversation as

song. Do you talk to people? Are you passionate in your interactions with your friends and loved ones? Coworkers? Most people use their words all day long with almost no preparation or preconception. We take this ability for granted. If you really want to get your point across when you're angry, you might stumble and search for the right words, you might make detours through some unwise and hurtful territory, but you are going to be clearly understood more often than not.

I see a clear connection between our ability to communicate in conversation and the necessary skills needed to write not just lyrics but music as well. The key and the struggle, I guess, is how do we become as confident in our ability to use that skill in a context outside conversation? For this, I have one simple exercise. Have a conversation. Find someone you can talk to with some degree of ease—friend, relative, drive-thru attendant—and ask them to interrogate you about your life, how you're feeling, what you fear. Record your conversation somehow. Let a little time pass and go back to it. Ideally you could take the time to transcribe at least your side of the conversation.

Now, look at what you said off the top of your head without any premeditation. Were you honest? Did you surprise yourself with any of your answers? Have you ever heard anyone sing any of the things you said? I'm willing to wager that you will recognize a similarity, at the very least, between how you speak and how songs are imagined. This is the real gift of human language and our desire to connect: that it works. And I'm convinced that if you can tell someone you love them and have them believe you, then you can write a song that's just as persuasive.

Here's a quick look at how you can use almost any snippet of conversation as a catalyst to generate some ideas. This is based on a transcript of a conversation with my brother-in-law, who writes about Hollywood for the most part but was interested in my creative process as I was preparing to write this book. Note that I've bolded the phrases that were most useful to me.

DANNY: **I've talked to some** actors **who don't want to talk** about their process . . .

JEFF: I'm not superstitious about it. It's possible that **talking** about it **might break the spell**. Maybe it's helpful for some people to think that it's not them—there are a lot of songwriters who think that they're just a conduit, that they're just channeling from **somewhere in the universe**. I don't think you need to think that way— obviously that helps some people—but I think it's just as interesting to say that that could be your subconscious.

DANNY: In reading your first book . . . **you don't** need to **worry about** talking about it, it's just about getting your ego out of the way.

JEFF: I don't think I'm free of that—**I think I'm getting** superstitious as we're talking. I don't want to say, "I've never had writer's block" because maybe I'm tempting my brain to rewire, "We're turning it off." But I do think those are self-fulfilling prophecies for some people: "I have writer's block." **Well,** when was the last time you picked up a pencil and tried to write without **wondering if it was** good or bad?

DANNY: For **me,** writer's block implies that you're victimizing yourself **from your** ego **point of view** of consciousness.

Now here are just the snippets together:

> *I've talked to some*
> *who don't want to talk*
> *talking might break the spell*
> *somewhere in the universe*
> *you don't worry about*
> *I don't think I'm free*
> *I think I'm getting well*
> *wondering if it was me*
> *from your point of view*

There are a million ways to rearrange just that one shard of communication. For the first example, I opted to not change the order of the words or add any "connecting tissue" words that would help make things rhyme or land in places where my brain was leading. But it's still pretty interesting as lyrics, right?

However, taking it a step further, and losing those "rules" might result in something like this . . .

> *I've talked to some who don't want to talk*
> *they think talking might break the spell*
> *somewhere in the universe you don't worry about*
> *where I wasn't free but I was getting well*
> *and as you left I started wondering*
> *if you would ever be able to tell*
> *there is a difference between you*
> *and me from your point of view*

To me both poem fragments are pretty singable, but loosening the rules added a layer of meaning.

The example above is what can happen with a pretty mundane and not particularly passionate conversational snippet. But what I'd really like to share with you is the type of intense loving discussion I think we all have when we're pushing our feelings against our vocabulary and struggling a bit to be understood. Which to me is even more songlike. An exchange that would illustrate how conversations are full of beautiful improvised language. I'll walk you through a song called "Guaranteed" that I put out on a solo album a few years ago. I think it contains a pretty good illustration of how a more intimate conversation can be appropriated for lyric writing. And how the way we really talk is more than enough poetically to make a song feel intimate and real and relatable. It came from a conversation between Susie, my wife, and me. I'll begin with the real conversation, as best as I can remember it . . .

JEFF: We've been through a lot, me and you.

SUSIE: Yeah, hospitals . . . bars . . .

JEFF: It has to suck sometimes dealing with me being such a weirdo. And being gone so much. And not knowing how to do "man" stuff.

SUSIE: You're no walk in the park!

JEFF: Right, maybe. But neither are you . . . Maybe that's a good place to start . . . ? Because when things go wrong, we have room to improve, it can get better, so our love gets stronger when we need it to.

SUSIE: How? I'd like to know how. And why does it have to be a reaction to tragic things happening?

JEFF: I think it's good that way. Isn't tragedy kinda guaranteed?

SUSIE: Yeah, but sometimes it just feels like it's too much. Doesn't it? Don't you ever start to think we can't go on when things are sucking so hard?

JEFF: Not really. Not anymore. I'm pretty sure, based on the evidence that we are still here, nothing can break you and me.

And then, from the finished lyrics . . .

We've been through a lot, me and you
Hospitals and bars
I know how it hurts
I'm a piece of work
And you're no walk in the park
Oh, that's a good place to start

When things go wrong
Our love gets stronger . . .

Oh, I'd love to know
How things go wrong
Love gets stronger each day . . .

Tragedy is guaranteed . . .

We think we can't go on
Nothing can break you and me

After all, when you're in a serious conversation, especially with someone you love, you search for language to express yourself. We're able to form really complex stories off the top of our heads. Conversation comes from our subconscious—we search for language, tell stories, express ourselves in a way that's organic. I think that's the starting point for writing anything. If you're able to express yourself as a human, you're able to mine that ability to create other modes of expression, to mine that ability for songs. To me, that's the best evidence that everyone can write a song. Maybe not everyone can make a chord progression, but everyone can make up a story.

13

EXERCISE 6:

Playing with Rhymes

I love rhyming. Sometimes an overly obvious rhyme scheme can become oppressive, and I have a real pet peeve about song lyrics that telegraph the impending rhyming word from a mile away. Country songs have a lot of trouble with this, in my opinion. I hate it when I can easily predict every rhyme in a song. There aren't a lot of hard and fast rules in terms of avoiding predictable rhymes, but I'm going to ask anyone reading this book to please, for the love of all things holy, not rhyme "train" with "rain" anymore. If you do, you better surround it with some of the best poetry ever written to cushion the blow.

One thing that I like to do and that I find scratches the same sort of itch that crossword puzzles can get to is writing freestanding rhyming couplets. "Freestanding" meaning that they are unattached to any poem or song.

Just taking two rhyming words and connecting them can be very satisfying, especially when you've freed yourself of the burden of the architecture and logic of an entire poem or lyric. As an example:

> *when Gwendolyn speaks to a county police*
> *plastic cup of beer held between her teeth*

It's not a perfect rhyme, but you get the idea. I can't wait to hear the rest of the song that fits in. I may never find it, but I enjoyed making that tiny little puzzle piece and I'm happy it exists.

Overall, these are just ideas and exercises to get you started, to get you excited about the music and rhythm of language. And speaking of music, hopefully you already have some melodies in your head as the result of experimenting with lyrics.

14

EXERCISE 7:

Don't Be Yourself

This might sound surprising, but you actually DON'T have to be yourself. Woody Guthrie's most famous bit of writing advice, and one that I think has been echoed by many other writers of all types, is, "Write what you know." I think it's fantastic advice. Especially in how it relates to the impulse a lot of young writers have to dig into tropes and ideas that don't bear much resemblance to the way they actually live their lives. A guy such as myself avoiding words like "glock" and "lambo," or phrases like "bottle of Jack" and "pick-'em-up truck," comes to mind when I consider how helpful this advice can be when applied correctly.

But let's face it, Woody Guthrie had a pretty rich and fascinating background to draw upon. So writing about what he knew really meant he could sidestep the relatively boring topics that are a big part of normal life today. Maybe he meant he wouldn't put on "airs" and try to sing about a debutante ball or something like that . . . actually, he probably could have, and he actually might have, now that I think about the varied manuscripts I have seen in his archives. Still, Woody got to be Woody, so it was pretty easy for him to say "write what you know."

Where does that leave the rest of us? The aspiring songwriters who didn't live through the Dust Bowl? Most of us have lives that are pretty far removed from the adventures and tales of survival we tend to value as authentic and interesting. While I agree it's important to be truthful about what affects you in your day-to-day living, I'd like to offer a solution to the stultifying feeling that our lives aren't worthy of songs being written about them: BE SOMEONE ELSE. Or something else. I'm not necessarily pushing for the wholesale invention of a new YOU Ziggy Stardust–type persona, even though that is an undeniably awesome approach if you can pull it off. I'm just saying it's worthwhile and helpful to consciously step outside of yourself from time to time and write from some "other" point of view.

I've done this my whole life. I think even before I wrote songs for myself to sing, I would write songs with the idea that someone else would be singing them. In Uncle Tupelo, I would always write with Jay Farrar's voice in mind, hoping that he would spare me the indignity of having to play the bass, which didn't come easy,

AND sing, which . . . how can I put this . . . did NOT come easy, especially when combined with playing bass. Even after I had made peace with my voice, I still had the strong impulse to write with the voice, life experience, and gravitas of other artists in mind. It really helped a lot of songs come out of me that I'm not sure would have made it through the dense neurotic thicket of self-doubt and insecurity that defined my own self-image. "Forget the Flowers" on *Being There* is a good example. Johnny Cash! That's what I was hearing in my head when I wrote that one. I still have to consciously try to sound like I'm not trying to sound like him when I sing that song.

This ability or desire to shift perspective just enough to let go of having to sound like me has been most useful in the work I've done writing for Mavis Staples's voice on and off throughout the last decade. But I think the most remarkable experience I've had working this way was during the writing process for the album *A Ghost Is Born*. At some point, I found myself trapped under the weight of my colossally screwed-up head and I couldn't bear the thought of singing another word as the entity known as Jeff Tweedy. Things were bad. I was a drug addict, I was dealing (or not dealing) with mental health issues . . . I'll assume you know most of the details, but to put it succinctly, I thought I was going to die and I was kind of OK with the idea. But I still really had a lot I wanted to get off my chest. Most important, I wanted my young children, my boys, Sammy and Spencer, to know me as the person I felt I truly was, and not really as the person I happened to have become. Reading to them was something I was still able to do with some reliability, and it occurred to me that children's books were almost all written from the point of view of animals or things, like caterpillars or trains. So I started writing songs to them from the point of view of animals, or at least with some element of an animal-like perspective. Which led to a semi-coherent Noah's ark concept that shaped the rest of the album. The song that may contain the most evident residue of the entire approach is "Company in My Back," written from the viewpoint of an insect at a picnic. That's the point of view that was in my mind, at least, but what it ended up being is far from impersonal. In fact, I find it to be heartbreakingly revealing when I read it or sing it today.

> *I attack with love, pure bug beauty*
> *I curl my lips and crawl up to you*
>
> *And your afternoon*
> *And I've been puking*

I think it's revealing because without the emotional cover of not being myself as the narrator of the song, I don't think I would have been secure enough to identify myself as something beautiful yet unwelcome. Like a bug at a picnic. An interloper. Facing danger bigger than anything I could ever imagine, and yet feeling gentle and deeply surrendered to the largeness of the world and its mysteries. Writing from a bug's place in the world allowed me to be honest, in other words. About things that were too painful to contemplate fully at the time.

Anyway, I think it's a helpful trick if you can get yourself to see the world from a new angle every once in a while. Look around the room you're in right now. What is the clock seeing from its perch on the mantel? Have you ever imagined what it's like to be a rug? How about a vacuum cleaner? Chaka Khan? Or maybe YOU could try your hand at writing a song in Johnny Cash's voice? That's the beauty of this approach: What you hear will never be the same as what I came up with. And it won't ever really be Johnny Cash or a paper wasp or a rotisserie chicken or an air conditioner . . . it's always going to still be you. And that's a great thing.

PART III

15

Pieces of Music

Start to Make Things

When I talked about my daily schedule, I talked about collecting pieces of language as a starting point, and I hope the exercises in the last section got you started—that you have a handful of lyrics, or phrases, or even a few words that you like. But along with those lyrics, it's also important to start collecting pieces of music. Riffs, bits of vocal melody, chord progressions, sounds, samples, loops, beats—basically anything in the sonic realm that you think you'd like to hear again and might be helpful in the construction of a song someday.

Since we're just talking about music, and since I don't read or write music (and even if I did, I don't think it would be fair to assume that you have that ability), this is quite a bit harder to write about than how I go about collecting lyrics is. So instead of exercises, I'll share more of a list of recommendations or suggestions—gentle nudges.

In some instances in this section, I'm going to have to assume you have some rudimentary knowledge of an instrument, or at the very least can carry a tune enough to present a melody that you can record or repeat in some way. Our early interactions with instruments are often some of the most freeing. Picking up my cousin's guitar and being able to play part of a Kansas riff on one string by sounding it out and trial and error is probably the single most important event of my life. But the relationship between those notes and the other strings on the guitar are where things get tricky and sometimes daunting, and I think it's important to stay in touch with that simple one-note mind-set. One-note-at-a-time melodic piano playing is another great place to calibrate your ear and reconnect with how fun and exciting it is to just plunk out a melody. And if you think it's impossible to make something interesting or beautiful with such a rudimentary technique, I'd like for you to go listen to "Know" by Nick Drake or "Rang Tang Ring Toon" by Mountain Man to hear how one string on a guitar or one note at a time is often just the right amount.

So hopefully you'll try it—even one string or one finger on a keyboard. But if even those aren't a part of your skill set yet, I hope that you'll still be able to absorb these recommendations as applicable toward a generalized atmosphere of making things, and that you'll find them easily amended or transposed to whatever mode of creativity you enjoy. And always try to keep in mind that what I *most* wish to convey is a broader definition of what a song is and can be to each of us in our lives and how much I feel we can all benefit from a day-to-day creative regimen.

16

RECOMMENDATION 1:
Learn Other People's Songs

We all have the ability to remember and record things that are important to us. A lot of people do it with pictures, obviously. I tend to do it with sound. I think sound has an underrated ability to evoke feelings. The way that people talk about aroma having an extraordinary power over our moods—sound does that for me, and I believe it probably does that for a lot of people. It could be a metal flagpole with a metal chain banging in the wind. It could be the way the wind is coming through the window in a hotel. It's a lot of things.

In my opinion, it's more important to be a good listener than to be a good musician. In fact, I wouldn't separate the two. I think the best musicians are the best listeners. I know there are a lot of musicians who can't play with a high level of physical aptitude or technique but who have made their worth known to the world through their ability to hear something nobody else has been able to. I think with a lot of jazz and ensemble-type music, you're terrible if you're not good at listening and only interested in what you're playing. It's like having a conversation with someone who's not listening to you— you want to kill that person.

Which brings me to other people's songs. Everyone I've ever met who has impressed me as a musician or a songwriter has also taught me about someone else's music besides their own. In a lot of cases by turning me on to new artists or recordings I'd never heard of. But also I've been enlightened by spending time listening to music with my musician friends and hearing it through their ears—by feeling the subtle shifts in breathing and body language as the sounds in the room cast a spell. What this has led me to understand and believe is that the best musicians are invariably the best listeners, and that they spend as much time maintaining their focus on other people's music as they do on their own. It seems like it would go without saying—the idea that if you want to learn how to do something, watch someone else do it, and watch them well.

Apprenticeships and oral traditions are a consistent part of many arts and crafts. But how do you watch someone write a song? First, you listen. Maybe you read the lyrics or try to play some of the notes yourself. But if you really want to get into the mind-set of a songwriter, you should learn other people's songs seriously and thor-

oughly. Tons of them. And don't stop. Ever watch someone crash and burn at a karaoke bar because they thought
they knew a song by heart but got lost even with the
words right in front of them? I love watching when that
happens because it reveals how even a simple, well-known
song can have a complexity and internal logic that didn't
happen just by accident. When they're well constructed,
finished songs often sound effortless, and I'm here to tell
you that takes work.

The easiest way to get a grip on how that happens is
to take the time to learn your favorite songs. Ideally,
learning a song well enough that you can perform it by
yourself is what I think is the most helpful. But even being able to confidently sing along without looking at a
lyric sheet is valuable if you want to get a sense of how
songs are paced and why certain song shapes are recur-
ring and satisfying. I still take time to learn and relearn
my favorite songs on a daily basis. I also spend a good
deal of time listening to new records, and old records
I've never heard before, in an ongoing search for songs
that inspire me to write my own. A big part of that inspiration comes through the process of taking them apart
enough to figure out how to play them on an acoustic
guitar and sing them to myself.

17

RECOMMENDATION 2:

Set a Timer

One of the main ways we cheat ourselves out of creating is the widely held belief that we need the right amount of time to make something of value—to make something worthwhile. We often resist a moment of inspiration because we're aware of a limited time window that might interrupt the flow and therefore think, "It's not even worth it to get started because I know I won't be able to finish it." This might be a valid excuse on a particular day or in a particular moment if your work ethic is solid otherwise and you're just temporarily missing a dependable way to document your ideas. In that case, it might even be a prudent way of avoiding a frustrating experience that could end up thwarting a pure impulse.

But let's face it: It's usually bullshit, right? It's pretty much garden-variety procrastination most of the time. Much of our ability to procrastinate, and to rationalize it, revolves around what we deem to be "ideal" circumstances in which to work. I'm not going to lecture you about the habit of putting things off. I do it myself quite frequently, and I'm aware that it's not necessarily always going to end in disaster or nothing getting done or a complete lack of progress. I do think, however, that the effort to counteract the desire to work only when the stars are aligned is a worthy one. Not to discount easily controlled conditions that enhance your level of ease and put you in the proper mind-set to get to work—a favorite beverage at hand, for example, or a certain type of notebook and pencil you enjoy the weight and feel of.

I have a favorite game I play to not just combat procrastination but also challenge the feeling that I should work only when I know it's going to be "good." This exercise helps keep my definition of what a song is, or can be, open and forgiving enough to allow pleasant anomalies to flourish.

It's a simple game. Basically, the whole gist is to set a timer for any amount of time you can spare (I think five to ten minutes is perfect) and tell yourself that whatever comes to you in that amount of time is a song. I even like to record what I come up with into my phone at the end of the time limit to really finalize the feeling that I met the challenge and stuck to the rules.

I came up with this practice on the road. I'm the kind of person who is always early. I know a lot of people think it's not very rock and roll to be punctual and courteous, but I disagree. I think manners are cool, and even revolutionary, and you won't convince me otherwise. So fuck you. Anyway, when you're always in the habit of being on time, you tend to spend a lot of time in hotel rooms packed up and ready to go ahead of schedule, just waiting for the call that the bus is there to pick everyone up. One day I wondered on a whim if the twenty minutes I had before lobby call was enough time to come up with and record a "finished" brand-new song.

So I set a timer on my phone and got out my guitar. After a few minutes I had something I was entertained enough by to start matching with lyrics, and at the end of the twenty minutes, I had written a song that I actually kind of loved. What really struck me about this experience was that I was certain that I had just made something that would never have existed without the limitations I had embraced, and also I had killed twenty minutes effortlessly. I can't say that this method has a high rate of success in terms of Top 40 hits or even songs that make it onto records, but it has happened—"You and I" for one—and for that I'm grateful. Actually, just having a useful coping mechanism for those moments of touring limbo fills me with gratitude.

18

Loosen Your Judgment

Maybe adding a time constraint to your songwriting isn't something that feels natural to you, or maybe you're still getting familiar with your instrument and it's a bit too daunting to think with a clock ticking. Or maybe time management and putting things off isn't a problem for you. If so, good for you, but you're going to have to find another way to shake things up and start writing, and I still would recommend learning to improvise a bit.

This is going to be an adjustment, especially for people who already respond well to order and structure. But it's worth it. So bang on a table and blurt out something primal. Play one chord and narrate your day so far. Just put something into a recorder. You've created something that didn't exist before—how freeing is that?

The important element here is that you find some

way to sidestep the part of your brain that wants perfection or needs to be rewarded right away with a "creation" that it deems "good"—something that supports an ideal vision of yourself as someone who's serious and smart and accomplished. Basically, you have to learn how to have a party and not invite any part of your psyche that feels a need to judge what you make as a reflection of you. Or more accurately, the part of you that cannot tolerate any outward expression that might be flawed.

Sadly, this part of who we are wields a lot of control over how much freedom we give ourselves to create. Many, many people I've known in my life have never truly gotten past this hang-up. Maybe I've met a few who have white-knuckled it enough to create an impressive body of work without letting go of judgment and control, but I must admit I always feel like I can hear a certain mirthless labor in their recordings. What I feel like I can sense is that they never got over having to sound bad to get good, and that they never really learned to embrace the joyousness of sounding "bad."

Actually, I think it's a skill that one would more likely relearn than learn. Kids are, in my experience, usually able to commit to creating in a way almost completely devoid of judgment. I love watching kids sprawled out on a carpet drawing or coloring. To me, it's the ideal creative state, and it's what I strive for more than any other aspect of what I do. It takes some work, and it takes tricks like the ones we've been discussing, but I've found it for myself, and it's worth it.

What I want you to find is what I've found through these practices: the thrill of "disappearing," as I'll call it, which I know I've talked about before but deserves another reminder here. I know I've achieved what I'm looking for in a creative experience when my sense of time and space has been altered—when I look up and all of a sudden it's three hours later and I'm a little surprised by where I am. It's those moments that give me the greatest satisfaction, and I find them to be extremely beneficial to my overall well-being. So much so that I decided to write this book because I truly believe that, at the very least, if you can unburden yourself of your more judgmental and discerning self with some regularity, you'll have a better life.

So what we're still talking about here are the different ways to trick yourself into letting your guard down. I'll admit I don't have all the answers. But I do think just naming the effort, and explaining it to yourself in these terms, can help. So here are a few more ideas to get you thinking about your own tricks that might work to point yourself in a freer direction, both in terms of music— our main topic here—and, as always, as part of the creative process in general.

You can do many other things to mix it up, like starting in the "wrong" place (more on that in the next part of the book). Or try a different tuning, which is mostly a tip for guitar players, but there are ways to alter some keyboards to provide some of the disorientation we're looking for. I do this all the time. Sometimes I detune a guitar until it makes an interesting chord voicing just by strumming the open strings. Then I might try a few normal chord shapes until I hear something I enjoy. This is an excellent thing to try if you're stuck in a rut of habitually putting your hands in the same place when you're trying to come up with a chord progression. Or when you're bored with the chord voicing you keep gravitating to. Sometimes these experiments result in songs that are specifically written for these alternate tunings, but frequently these moments of disorientation lead me to something new that I can transpose back into standard tuning.

Another thing you can try is a different instrument. Same principle as above. Sometimes I feel like I know what I'm going to hear when I pick up my guitar, and it feels a little dull and predictable. A G chord again? Yawn. I'm not joking here. I've been unthinkingly playing a G chord every time I pick up a guitar for going on forty years! One way I get around this is by sitting down with an instrument I'm not very confident on, like a piano or a banjo. Synthesizers are awesome tools for shaking things up. There are even a lot of music-making apps for phones that I've really enjoyed exploring. All these new experiences outside your comfort zone will give you musical ideas you never would have thought of without challenging yourself to listen to what happens when you have no idea what's going to happen. You just have to be ready and open to it.

19

RECOMMENDATION 4:

Steal

Yes. You read that correctly. I am going to openly encourage theft in a book based on our shared ability to create and the notion that anyone can write a song. Isn't stealing wrong? Yes, absolutely wrong!

Perhaps "stealing" isn't an accurate description of what I'm suggesting. However, I chose "stealing" because that's the word that feels the most honest and liberating and enticing. The point is, I don't think you should be afraid to use the direct influence of someone else's work, even though we've been taught that it's wrong to take something without permission. This practice is perfectly in keeping with the underlying premise of a SHARED ability to create.

Everyone who you could possibly steal from at this point in human evolution is a thief. Even innovators seemingly without any historical precedent are found to be building on someone else's foundation, upon deeper investigation. Rock and roll music, as an example, is thought of as an explosion of new ideas and wildly individual expression. But when you zoom in, the brazenness of each song and performance style lies more in *how* it was stolen outright and shamelessly appropriated with devilish delight. Ideas weren't as closely guarded and protected as intellectual property, for better or worse.

I should probably steer myself away from a sociopolitical tangent here, but I think it would be irresponsible not to point out how copyright laws and the ways they're enforced have changed based on how certain minority-innovated art forms became culturally and commercially valuable. But I digress . . .

So for this chapter, here's the gist: I do think it would be wrong to take someone else's song and, without making it your own in any way, present it as your own work. However, almost anything short of that extreme has artistic validity, in my point of view. With caveats. I think anything left unchanged (choruses, riffs, etc.) should always be credited, and I think it's always important to share your inspirations when given the opportunity. But that still leaves an enormous world of musical ideas to inspire and integrate into your own ideas. Here are some of the ways I use outside influences overtly and consciously.

Chord Progressions

A lot of times when I fall in love with a new song, my first impulse is to learn it on the guitar. What I tend to be drawn to the most is how chord progressions can work in unexpected ways against a vocal melody. When I come across chord pairings and passages of chords that are surprising or new to me, I often play them into my phone without the vocal melody or with a new vocal melody added to obscure the source.

Then later, when I come across these musical ideas in my voice memos, if I am still able to recall the song being referenced, I'll discard it as a potential building block for my own song, or I'll spend more time figuring out some way to make the chordal transitions that intrigued me more my own. More often, I find that what I've recorded has lost the original flavor of the song it's "stolen" from and I'm left with an exciting morsel that I can season to taste. Recently I fell in love with a song called "Andromeda" by the artist Weyes Blood. The song sounds a lot like its name—celestial and luminous. Think Karen Carpenter's kid sister high on edibles. I had to learn it. From just that one song, I found three wonderfully unexpected chord changes that really heightened my appreciation of the song. And I should tell you, it inspired me to write three songs using these changes that sound absolutely nothing like "Andromeda" by Weyes Blood.

Samples

A lot of better sources are out there if you're looking for info on how to incorporate samples into your songwriting process, but I just want to include this suggestion as an unreserved endorsement of their use in the creation of exciting new art.

Melodies

The reappropriation of a melody is a trickier business when it comes to the legal questions that might crop up if you're making commercially available art. But I believe that writing your own lyrics to an existent melody is a damn fine thing to do if you don't have much of a handle on the music side of things and you really need to get something off your chest in song. There are songs in the public domain that you can do anything you like with, of course. But I say go for it—tell the harrowing tale of coming out to your parents set to the tune of "Poker Face" by Lady Gaga if need be. Get that shit out of you. Don't wait for the music side to catch up if you have a story to tell. That's what I think.

PART IV

20

Can You Hear
What Comes Next?

This next step is where things get borderline mystical for a lot of people when they try to explain how a song happens—how words and music join together to form something greater than the sum of their parts.

I'm not sure I can demystify something I feel wholly inadequate to explain. For me, the moments that make my scalp tingle a bit are when I hear myself sing a lyric out loud for the first time. On occasion I make myself cry. Not because I'm marveling at my songwriting genius or I'm overcome with my poetic gifts. It's a moment that feels more like I'm witnessing something better than me, or better than what I imagined I could make, being born. Certain things I've written that at first didn't strike me as remotely worthy of being sung have, when sung for the first time, startled me by uncovering truths about myself I had no intention of revealing. Recently I finished a song with the lyric "She holds my hand between her knees / Like a dream I'm never sure what it means." It's kind of songwriterly cute in a way I might otherwise feel a little self-conscious about. Except when I sang it out loud for the first time, I felt a composite memory wash over me: When the lights would dim at basement rec-room get-togethers in junior high school and my classmates began pairing off in the shadows, I would always find myself paralyzed on the couch holding some small, adorable, sweaty hand, 100 percent convinced that the very clear signals I was receiving were all in my imagination and not to be trusted. Slow on the uptake, I was.

Sometimes the words hang in the air in an almost physical way, as if they've taken on the properties of an actual object I could touch and feel if I reached out. Or like the feeling you have when you know someone has entered a room you've been occupying alone. And even though they make no sound nor announce themselves, you can sense their presence and that you're no longer alone.

The surprising thing is that sometimes I don't even always love the songs that provide these exquisite moments when I hear them later. But out of all the things I enjoy about making up songs, those moments mean the most to me. In fact, I wouldn't be writing this book if I didn't believe that those experiences are so valuable that it would be wrong to not at least encourage everyone to have their own.

So, to me, that's ONE song. The one you've been working on, the one that's the goal of writing and reading this book. You'll know it when you have it. If that can happen to you singing to yourself, it has a pretty good chance of working for someone else. I might have to write fifty songs or almost-songs to get one, or sometimes I might get a string going where I feel supernaturally in touch with my abilities.

Am I contradicting myself here? If a song is conjured more than it's crafted with intent, why have we been learning all these exercises, doing all the work step-by-step? Because hopefully all of what I've been sharing here is in service of your reconnecting with your imagination in a way that will eventually allow you to simply close your eyes and *imagine* what comes next.

It is possible to write a song in the time it takes to play it. To start with just an idea and play through like you're listening to a record. How? That sounds crazy. It doesn't happen that way very often, even for me. But the only way I ever got to that point was because I learned these other avenues into my subconscious and then made well-worn paths, eventually becoming conversant enough with what I like to hear and what kinds of shapes songs come in that I could improvise a passable song the way you might use your language skills to describe your day.

Can you do that? With practice, I bet you can! I don't think I'm that special, and I believe that's what can happen when you keep doing everything we've covered so far again and again—you stop having to work at it and it just comes to you. Early on, trial and error plays a much bigger role in how words and music come together, and there are always going to be moments that require some patience. But the more you stick with it, the easier it will become to just close your eyes and listen to the music in your head and imagine what you'd like to hear next. Also, importantly, it will become easier to determine when an idea isn't working, as opposed to an idea that is maybe just one ingredient away from being magical. That requires a lot of practice and work.

By the way, I'd like to add that you don't have to do any of these particular exercises—though without the daily-discipline component, you might just have to be happy with writing a few songs a year that come to you in intermittent bursts of inspiration.

So let the magic happen. It's almost time! But first, let's take a step back and look at some of the practical ways a song can be constructed out of the ideas we've stockpiled in the previous chapters. Basically, start by finding one of the melodies or chord progressions you've collected that you feel drawn to finish, and then scan through your lyrical ideas for something that fits rhythmically and emotionally. If you can't find anything, go back and work through the lyrical exercises that are related to tailoring words to a melody, like finding words on a page. Easy, right?

OK, just because the description of a process sounds mundane doesn't mean that the end result will be. In fact, I probably complete more songs in this manner than any other. It occurs to me as I write this that my idea of a song might be drastically different from yours, and I might be leading you through some peculiar-feeling maze toward a rather nebulous and ill-defined goal. Good! I think you should be suspicious of my idea of a song as well as your own preconception about how you go about making the songs you think you want to write. I'm even willing to say that the songs you don't know you want to write are better than the ones you're picturing.

Nothing about the way I enjoy my own creative endeavors made much sense to me early on. I knew I had an instinct for songwriting and a desire to learn, but because the reading-music part was so difficult and my aptitude on an instrument was lagging, I'd always assumed I'd never know how people actually write songs. Then I read something somewhere about how Inuit carvers create. As I understand it, they take a walrus tusk or a piece of limestone, and they don't think, "I'm going to carve an elk or a seal or an eagle." They simply carve, and let the material tell them what it wants to become. They believe its essence was there all along, and that they just opened it up and revealed it. Getting from the nonsense syllables of a mumble track to a finished lyric through multiple revisions mirrors this process for me. The melody being the stone or ivory. I focus on just the sounds at first, carving toward words, and then words with meaning, until an image appears and finally I can add clear, precise language that underlines and reveals a "moose" or an "otter"—which, in my case, of course, is almost invariably a song about "death."

That's what I'm like when I'm in my most ideal state of creativity: I'm as excited about seeing what happens next as if I were watching myself do it. Again, I'm going to repeat how this is the part I think I can encourage and teach. The processes I'm pushing can be used over and over, and they'll never result in the song you're picturing. If you use the exact same process I used to write "I Am Trying to Break Your Heart," you won't write "I Am Trying to Break Your Heart (Again)" or even "I Am Trying to Break Your Heart (Tokyo Drift)." And I know this for a fact because I've used these processes over and over for years and I'm still delighted and surprised at the different shapes and animals they unlock from the dull stone that is my brain.

The creative state is the most important part. None of it means anything if you're not excited by the discovery of what you're making.

21

Recording What You've Done

Listening to Your Own Voice

It's almost impossible to work on songs without recording yourself at some point. Even people with the ability to notate music make simple demo versions. I've always been happy with a simple recording of a solo acoustic performance as a demo to build on later. Early on, before iPhones, I used a cheap dictaphone tape recorder. Some of these recordings have even been released over the years.

Now I'm totally content with digital voice memos on my phone. But I've wondered if I would be as content if I were just beginning to learn how to write songs now. Early in my recording career, my voice was a major inhibiting factor in how secure I felt while recording, and it affected my ability to focus on the song itself versus the performance. The crappy tape machine I had solved this problem for me by making my voice sound . . . not

like my own voice, exactly. The pitch control was out of
whack just enough to make my voice warblier and a bit
distorted. I loved it. My voice was altered just enough for
me to be able to listen without hearing my perceived flaws
and insufficiencies.

A digital voice memo is always much less forgiving
and accurate, and I'm lucky that I've made peace with
my singing voice over the years. But what would I do if
I were starting again? Well, first of all, if you don't want
to listen to yourself, don't. The process and experience of
conjuring a song is more important than listening to recordings of yourself.

However, I would like to point out to anyone troubled by the sound of their own voice that your voice is
your body, so you have to at least tolerate it. It's important to work toward acceptance at a minimum and love as
a goal. In the meantime, here are a few tips for recording
yourself that might ease some of the glare and shock of
getting used to hearing a recording of your singing voice.

1. Take the time to find a nice-sounding room to record
   in. Bathrooms are generally excellent because of all the
   sound-reflecting surfaces. Lots of professional recordings have been done in bathrooms, and almost all sing-
   ers prefer their voice with at least a little reverb.

2. Be conscious of where you place your microphone.
   This is surprisingly overlooked by even seasoned song-

writing veterans. If you're recording into a phone, learn where to place it to get the balance between your instrument and voice that you find most satisfying. If you're recording just your voice, find a distance from the microphone that gives you at least a little room atmosphere to cushion the edges of a digitally recorded and unadorned melody.

3. Experiment with different recording methods and types of vocal processing. This advice is a bit out of my own personal wheelhouse because I've avoided using home recording software and multitracking equipment (of which there are a ton of reasonably priced options) in the songwriting process almost as a principle for as long as it's been available. I find it difficult to keep my focus on the song when there are more knobs to push and twiddle with than just Record and Stop. Even in the studio, I resist touching knobs because I sense that I've stopped listening to the whole picture the second my fingers touch a control. My attention seems to be immediately diverted to thinking only about the parameter I am now "controlling." But that's me and my quirks. I have tons of musician and songwriting friends and acquaintances who have a lovely time self-engineering much more elaborate home recordings. Maybe you'd enjoy that aspect, and I don't want to steer you away from it. It would certainly provide someone uncertain about their voice with an

almost-infinite array of technological vocal disguises to clear a path forward.

— Mumble Tracks —

Another scenario: What do you do when you have a melody you like and a good idea of where the chords go, and you're eager to get to work on an arrangement, but you don't have the words yet? When you have inspiration but no lyrics yet, and don't want to waste the energy you're feeling by shutting down your musical impulses while your language center catches up?

I'll tell you what I and a lot of other songwriters do in these circumstances. Fake it! I sing nonsense that fits the melody and that has the right sounds in the right places, so I can get a better picture of what the overall song is going to feel like when I find the words that complete the picture. I call them "mumble tracks," and if you've listened to a lot of Wilco, you've probably heard a few that have been inadvertently left in the final mix because I never found actual words that meant as much to me as the way my nonsense sounds made me feel. Honestly! Not to toot my own ridiculous horn here, but I've gotten so good at making my mumbled singing sound like words that I've played mixes for people and afterward had them compliment me on the lyrics! Sometimes when

I look at them in disbelief, they'll even quote their favorite lines back to me (as I take dictation, naturally).

How these mumble tracks end up as finished "Grammy Award–winning" lyrics is a process I think anyone could figure out with a little practice. To me, the key is to surrender to the nonsense and write down the first words that come to your mind as you listen back to what you've recorded. It can take some repetition, but eventually it stops sounding like gibberish and it starts feeling almost like you're translating from another language—or even better, like you're taking dictation. Once that step is out of the way, I sit down with just the words on the page to see if there is any sense at all to be made out of the raw translation. Shockingly, there is almost always more sense being made than anyone would anticipate. I've even had some lyrics come out fully formed from the first translation. I'm not smart enough to figure out how to account for that seemingly implausible feat, but I swear it has happened.

Most of the time, however, it takes many revisions to squeeze something coherent and singable out of the process, but boy is the payoff worth the effort. It's such a wonderful feeling when it all falls into place and leaves me once again with a bemused "How did I do that?" sensation. I kind of breezed past a word a sentence or two ago that I think it would be a shame not to draw more attention to—"singable." The main advantage of being able to free yourself enough to basically semi-scat over your songs is the way this emphasizes how you want the melody to sound over the idea that the words you've written are perfect. You might then discover that you need to alter the melody or add a syllable to a few vowel sounds here and there. This is the best way I've found to keep my mind focused on how a lyric "sings" and phrasing.

What I've found after writing reams of songs in almost every conceivable manner is that I tend to WANT to sing the songs that were worked on this way more than those from other styles of writing. Something else worth noting is that I can almost always get the lyrics to say what I want them to say even if I have to take out a favorite word or phrase because it's hard to sing or just lands in an odd way that clanks against the ear.

Spending so much of life using this technique has, I think, also given me a better sense of whether something is going to be pleasant or satisfying to sing no matter how the lyrics are generated. Here's a real tip to remember as a songwriter: If you don't like what you're singing, and how it feels to sing it, and how it sounds to your ear, you have no reason to expect anyone else will want to sing along with you. Isn't that the point of all this in a way? Don't we want more than anything to make something that reflects who we are and how we feel honestly enough that someone else might feel seen or acknowledged, and less alone?

22

Are You Stuck?

How to Get Past "Writer's Block"

Hopefully, you've already had the magical experience of a whole song, or a portion of one, coming together in a way that feels exciting. And maybe you've even recorded it and heard yourself sing it. But if not? I guess now is the time to admit that I've always been skeptical of the term "writer's block." Not because I've never experienced a period when I've felt unproductive or uninspired. But because I recognized that it isn't really a block; it's a judgment. Because it's rare that you can't make anything. I don't believe a writer ever truly loses the ability to create. But all writers go through periods when they don't like what they're creating as much as they wish they did. Of course I'm stating the obvious: It's well known that the sensation of being blocked is a psychological issue, and I'd like to share some of my thoughts and insights about where our thinking gets distorted when we get stuck.

First off, let's stop calling it a "block." The only im-
pediment between a creator and their goal is actually a
creation in itself. So we can name it whatever we like. I
prefer to think of these periods as hurdles or speed bumps
or challenges. Calling it a "block" seems to give it way
more weight than it deserves. It's odd that we don't tend
to give our other internal mental states such solid physical metaphors. "My new song is a sun-dappled pond—
dive in!" Says no one. The main problem with calling it a
"block," though, is how it implies that forward is the only
direction we're allowed to move—that what is on the
other side of that monolith is the only place we want to
be and the only goal worth striving for. This is all nonsense. And once again, everything you find enticing
about being able to circumvent your "blocked" state is
also a product of your imagination. When I feel like I'm
stuck, I try to put myself back in touch with the reality of
the situation. There are no rules AND I make them! Here
are some ways to reaffirm your place in the hierarchy of
your own imagination.

— Start in the Wrong Place —

Starting in the wrong place is a good message, and turns
your judgment upside down. If you like delicate, melodic songs, maybe start with a drum machine. If you're

pretty sure your chorus sucks, start with it; make it the beginning of the song and see if you feel differently about it. Can you play the chord progression in the reverse order? It's amazing how this can work sometimes. I've reversed chord progressions without having to alter a melody except slightly. Did you write the song on an acoustic guitar? Play it loud on an electric.

— Start in the Right Place —

Let's say you're stuck trying to finish a song. Do you have a favorite part? A favorite lyric? Start there. This is one of the most helpful bits of advice I've ever given to myself. Without rearranging my songs this way, I never would have learned the power a first line can have over the trajectory of an entire song. When I come across a good line, I almost always put it first. In fact, I'd say a good first line is the most determining factor in whether a song I've written sees the light of day. "The ashtray says / You were up all night," "When you're back in your old neighborhood / The cigarettes taste so good," "I'm surprised staring at the knives / Lying silent in the drawer." All of those lines, to me, carried enough imagery and intrigue to propel me into the rest of the song. So, lose the restraint. Songs aren't generally paced like novels or short stories, even. They're often more like bumper stickers. If you have a lyric that feels great to sing and grabs your attention, see what happens when you open up with that line. It's such a simple thing, but it's startling how transformative it can be. At the very least, it's a great way to dismantle whatever barrier is tormenting you. Kind of like, "OK, I can't climb over this wall in front of me, but how about this CHOCOLATE CAKE?"

— Put It Away —

This advice might not make sense if you aren't interested in being a person who writes songs as a part of a daily routine. But this is a great tip for anyone not working on a deadline—which should be just about anyone writing a song. Put away whatever you're working on that you find frustrating. Don't think about it. Leave it alone. Maybe take one last crack at it before you go to bed to see if your brain can untie some of the knots while you're asleep. Which, again, is something I recommend trying with any creative work you're involved in—stuck or not.

But do yourself a favor and find an activity that helps you push the reset button on your brain. Sometimes it feels like a wall only because you're banging your head on it. For me, believe it or not, I like to work on a different song or start a new one. That's the advantage of making crafting songs a daily endeavor. I always have a backlog of unfinished songs to dig up and think about when I set aside one I'm stymied by. A good number of the unfinished songs I have lying around are songs that I've put away in frustration, and it's been incredible to me how often they seem to work themselves out when you avert your expectant gaze.

Sometimes it's good news, and the songs are way more done than I thought they were. But it isn't always good news. With the benefit of time, I can see that what I was asking of some songs was far from what their nature would allow. But either way, being reminded of how songs have a life of their own will often send me right back to the troubled song I just stepped away from with a newfound appreciation for what I have in front me versus what I was aiming for.

One of the ways anyone can get better at songwriting is by learning to accept what is given, even if it feels like it came from nowhere. What I mean by that is, sometimes we become overly suspicious of things that are easy. Things we're "good at" can be devalued in unfair ways sometimes. I think it's natural to strive to be great and equally natural to imagine that greatness requires struggle and even pain. But that belief often forces us to look down on the things that feel effortless. I went through a period where I was embarrassed by the country and folk songs I was writing, which I didn't ask myself to write and which seemed to flow out of me unprovoked.

But at some point, I figured out that I was a lot more productive when I just went with it instead of trying to figure out how to turn a three-chord folk song into a prog-rock song.

In a way, our album *The Whole Love* begins and ends at the two poles of this revelation. I didn't set out to illustrate this transition in song sensibilities explicitly, but going from the opening track, "Art of Almost," to the closer, "One Sunday Morning," really is a good way to see what I'm getting at here. I'm still excited by the recordings and arrangements of both songs, even though they couldn't be more divergent stylistically.

The truth is they started in almost exactly the same place. Both songs are simple three- or four-chord folk songs. Somewhere in the process of making that album, it occurred to me that not all of my simple songs were surviving the maximalist approach to arranging we had applied to "Art of Almost." It's a lesson I think I've needed to learn and relearn more than a few times over the years but it really is a valuable one. Don't undervalue things that come easy. Sometimes they're the things that would be the hardest for someone else to do and often they are the things that would be almost impossible to do when you try too hard.

Having said that, I'm kind of glad I went through those "square peg/round hole" periods. It makes things interesting and I enjoy those songs now, but I sure wouldn't recommend it as a healthy way to work. Let me just say this: I believe we stop ourselves sometimes when we're happy. We create conflict in our relationships sometimes because we're feeling uncertain and needy. Feeling attached to something can be uncomfortable. Sometimes you're stuck because you're anxious about losing something you love. Maybe you were sailing along working on a song and you kind of fell in love with it. And then you felt vulnerable because "What if it's not really good?" Or "What if I can't realize the full potential of this song?" Isn't that what someone in the world of psychology would call an "unhealthy attachment"? Maybe you pulled back when you started to feel something. Maybe you recognized yourself in the song and felt a connection that felt like love. And then you worried, "Will it love me back?" Just let a song be itself. Let it be what it wants to be—what it needs to be. A song will always love you back, but sometimes it just needs a little space.

Don't Put It Away

Now that I've promoted the idea that a helpful move when stuck is to walk away for a while, I'd like to make a not entirely contradictory suggestion. Keep punching. Sit in the discomfort you're feeling and will your song into being.

In the previous paragraphs, I stressed the point that

a lack of struggle doesn't have to mean the work isn't serious or worthy. I believe that's an important point to make because most people intuit that difficulty equals quality—the idea that it *must* be hard to write a good song. We needed to get that line of thinking swept aside, primarily because it's much more prevalent. Done? Great.

Now let's discuss the truth behind what hard, persistent work and a determined outlook can do for you. There are those among us who lose their nerve when things become difficult. Let's face this head-on. Ample excuses will always be available when you're talking yourself out of making any work of art. Number one, "Who needs it?" I mean, it's not like you're clocking out at the sandwich shop while there's a line out the door. You're not a surgeon with an exposed heart beating in front of you that you've just decided isn't really worth the bother today. It's a song. So what? Well, fucker, here's so what! Giving up becomes a habit. And the delayed gratification that comes from a song finished with some hardship is going to teach you more about writing songs than this entire book will ever be able to impart. Through your own grit and effort, you will learn where you're likely to trap yourself in dead ends, and you'll be one more song wiser to the idea that songs all happen the same way.

Not to mention how great it feels to be able to say "I did it. I didn't give up. That song now exists. And now

I'd like to thank the Grammy committee and my agent and . . . oh yeah, God. Even though I really don't think God had much to do with it . . ." Anyway, all future procrastination will be a tiny bit less persuasive in the wake of one hard-won song, right?

23

What Did You Just Make? Is It Any Good?

Does It Need to Be Good?

I'm hoping that by this point you have something—in your head, in your digital recorder, in a notebook, somewhere. But is it any good? This is obviously an important question. We build our lives around wanting to be good at something and our desire to have our contributions recognized. So I'm not going to argue that it shouldn't matter to you whether the song you make is good. But I will argue that how you judge the art you make is nowhere near as important as the act of creation itself.

And it's going to be a tough assignment if you only want to make "good" songs. I want to stress again that it's necessary to learn how to be OK with being bad at what you do—sound bad, write a bad song, suck at playing the guitar—or you'll never get to "good." And you have to keep being OK with going through "bad" to get to "good."

So you might as well try to find the joy in creating even a bad song or a bad poem or a bad painting or whatever art you need to make. We could all use a break from our egos—from the ever-vigilant, constantly observing, hypercritical part of our brains we rely on to protect us from ever having our feelings hurt or any type of psychic injury. You know who didn't have that when they were a kid? You. Nobody has that until a certain age. I get why we need to protect ourselves, and how having the ability to put a squad of brain cells functionally in charge of patrolling the perimeter must provide some evolutionary advantage to survival. But it does a lot less for our quality of life.

We lose a lot as we grow older, and that apparatus becomes more efficient and adept at dismissing our own fantastic and childish whims and desires. Maybe it starts when we learn that we are separate from the world. That everything that surrounds us isn't just a part of who we are—that there are "others," that everything isn't only for us, and that those others might have wants and desires that outweigh our own. Maybe it starts when we learn that we need to be discerning in who we pick as friends— when we start to question motives and when we become suspicious of other people's thoughts.

I'm sure someone knows the answer to when and why we forfeit our wonderful innocence and become self-conscious and harsh judges of ourselves. All I know is that kids are invariably better artists than adults are and more in touch with their creativity, too. Imaginations run wild when you get down on the floor to color with some toddlers. Talk about inspiring! Ask a little kid to tell you about a painting they're working on. It's a miraculous thing. And I don't think it's unreasonable to aspire to that level of artistic liberation. I believe it's still there in all of us. I wrote about this in my first book, but I think it's worth emphasizing: During my stay in a mental hospital some sixteen years ago now, I witnessed this childlike superpower reassert itself, take hold, and transform a woman who was virtually catatonic in an art-therapy class. I think about it almost every day.

A sixty-something heroin addict who had spent the better part of the previous thirty years in and out of institutions and living on the streets—and whom I had not heard make a sound in any of the group therapy sessions, or even in the smoking room—drew a simple picture of herself. It wasn't great. But it looked like her.

When she held it up for the class to see, I heard her voice for the very first time. She said she couldn't remember the last time she had held a pencil. She smiled! And cried. Everyone clapped and gathered around to hold her. It was such a stark, amazing, healing thing to see someone's eyes light up—become human again—when they realized they had the power to make something that wasn't there.

It's a power that we reserve for "God"—to manifest things out of thin air. How incredible is that? Close your eyes and imagine the color blue or a sound. How did you do that? You created that. That's not the same sound someone else is going to make. We discount that as something we're supposed to measure against other people's imaginations, and that's a squandered gift.

I don't like every song I write, but I like that I wrote it. I know that for every five or so songs I write, I'm going to have one that means a lot to me, and it wouldn't have come to me if I hadn't written the other four songs, if I hadn't practiced getting to that place. A place that's as close to coloring on the floor as I can get.

24

Sharing Your Song

Now that you wrote a song, what are you going to do about it? Do you have to record it beyond the voice memo, or a demo you made, to perform it? Maybe not! I have one strong suggestion to make. But let's take a look at a few options first. I'm realizing as I write this that I'm starting to envision a whole other tome on all the vagaries and subtle indignities of being in a band—maybe I'll call it *Being in a Band*; that's a vast, vast topic to me. And now I'm reminded of how my father would habitually bring up what he had "a hankerin' for" for his next meal with his mouth full of his evening supper. So . . . I'll keep this book in the realm of being a solitary pursuit.

Let's define a song here, in the context of this book, as being something you create and perform by yourself. Here's my strong suggestion: Play your song at least once for at least one person other than yourself. Allow yourself to feel the intimacy and vulnerability of singing your song out loud. With someone listening—preferably someone you love. I used to play my songs for my mother. But it could be anyone. Open mic? I think a pet could even qualify. The important part is that it's a consciousness outside of your own.

This isn't quite the old trope about a tree falling in woods. I don't think your song doesn't exist until you manifest it in someone else's imagination. But I do think that what makes a song a song is how it feels when it's sung. You might give up halfway through. You might change the words as you're singing them the way you would when you anticipate someone you're speaking to isn't quite following. Because every song should make some effort to connect. Songs are pleas. It's all about reaching out and pulling in . . . or pushing out and look-ing in—in equal and unequal amounts. To whatever degree you need that connection in your life, you've at least taken the time and made the effort to create a song. I would love for you to have the full weight of this one simple truth rest on your shoulders gently for long enough to understand what it is you've done.

ACKNOWLEDGMENTS

I'd like to thank Danny Miller, my wonderful brother-in-law, for helping me get the ball rolling. Tom Schick and Mark Greenberg for their insight and near-constant support. Josh Grier, Crystal Myers, Dawn Nepp, and Brandy Breaux for keeping my life and work manageable. My dear family for making everything worthwhile. And Jill Schwartzman for once again tricking me into thinking I can write a book and then proving it to me.

Also, I would like to mention my undying gratitude to all of the songwriters and artists I've learned from and continue to be inspired by. Without your work, my work would not exist and I live to continue passing along whatever spark I can to keep that light burning for those who follow.

ABOUT THE AUTHOR

As the founding member and leader of the Grammy Award–winning American rock band Wilco, and before that the cofounder of the alt-country band Uncle Tupelo, **Jeff Tweedy** is one of contemporary music's most accomplished songwriters, musicians, and performers. Jeff has released two solo albums, written original songs for eleven Wilco albums, and is the author of the *New York Times* bestseller *Let's Go (So We Can Get Back): A Memoir of Recording and Discording with Wilco, Etc.* He lives in Chicago with his family.